YOGA WITH A FRENCH TWIST

A Journey through the Chakras

Wishing you Joy, Love & Peace,

Christine H. Griggs

Christine Griggs

This book is dedicated to my brother Patrice,
who taught me to live the life I was meant to have.

True Yoga is not about the shape of your body but the shape of your life. Yoga is not to be performed. Yoga is to be lived.

—Aadil Palkhivala

Contents

INTRODUCTION

Yoga is like Music;
The Rhythm of the Body,
The Melody of the Mind,
The Harmony of the Soul.
It creates the Symphony of Life.

—B.K.S. Iyengar

Can you hear the music within you?

Has the rumble of notes trying to escape from deep within you grown more insistent lately? Do you hear it during your waking hours and during your dreams: the strings of the violins, the beating of the drums... begging you to set them free?

Your life has been a succession of hopes and dreams fulfilled into exquisite concertos or discordant cacophonies, as well as numbing grief and loss woven into soulful sonatas, but do you feel that you have unheard music left in you? Do you feel that you have yet to write your symphony?

Your soul is desperately trying to get your attention.

Listen.

When you finally hear its voice, magic happens. The world is brighter, not just for you, but for everyone around you.

Because when you find your music, the whole universe smiles.

When you share your music, the whole universe dances.

This book is a symphony of love as I lay bare the most vulnerable stories of my life and share their lessons to guide you on your journey.

This book is about helping you to recognize the voice within, helping you to connect the notes so you can write your symphony and make the world dance.

This book is about my soul speaking to your soul.

Sharing the wisdom of an ancient tradition that has helped me to connect the notes.

An ancient tradition that means union.

Yoga.

YOGA

I discovered yoga later in life, in my early forties.

Physically, I had just run a marathon and knew I needed to stretch more.

Spiritually, the message of the church I had been attending was not fulfilling me, and I had been on a soul journey with my best friend. Our studies of Eastern philosophy—yoga and Buddhism—had left me craving more.

Honestly, I didn't really know what to do about it; yoga was not as prevalent in Tidewater Virginia then as it is now when it seems that a new studio opens monthly. I was not ready to go out of my way to practice yoga and from what I had seen of yoga studios on television or in magazines, they did not appeal to me. Sitting still and chanting was not my cup of tea.

But, as the saying goes, *when the student is ready the teacher will appear.* One morning as I finished my daily workout at the gym on our military base, I happened to see a small flyer hidden behind Army leaflets. It was advertising yoga classes. The yoga classes were held there twice a week and, best of all, they were free.

I showed up ten minutes early the following evening, uncertain but eager. I was welcomed by Craig, a cheerful middle-aged man with a twinkle in his eye who looked like Santa Claus.

Craig taught with his eyes closed. He used to tell me he didn't care what the students did; he just taught his class. I think this helped me to get over all my insecurities about "doing it right." If my first teacher had been "hands-on" and picky about the poses themselves, I probably would not have stayed. His approach helped me to grow at my own pace and, through this process, find the stillness within me.

The stillness that scared me.

My practice grew of its own accord. I had other teachers, other guides, "yoga friends" who, each in their own way, enriched my journey. All the puzzle pieces of my life were coming together and I could finally see the whole picture in all its beauty.

I could see myself, not the little scattered pieces of me, but the whole radiant truth of who I was.

I could hear the music.

When I am silent, I fall into a place where everything is music.

—Rumi

I now teach yoga and train yoga teachers, both of which would have seemed bizarre several years ago. As my mother pointedly asked: "You're a trained translator, why do you want to teach yoga?"

Because this was the crossroad where my path led me and I took the "yoga turn."

Because I had been continuously running longer and harder— figuratively and metaphorically—and needed to hit the pause button. You can only run so many marathons on the track and in your life.

Because I needed to take care of myself—body and mind—in a different way, and help others do the same.

* * *

Yoga is a choice that nurtures your life.

Yoga doesn't change you per se; it just highlights what already *is*, all that is good, vibrant and beautiful in you, all of your gifts.

It allows you to discover the music within.

It enhances the colors and nuances that make you *you*.

It allows you to see and live the IMAX 3D version of your life.

It gives you the clarity to see what has always been there, the strength to unearth it and the courage to show it to the world.

As I always tell my students, yoga is not an end in itself.

Yoga is union.

Yoga is life.

Yoga is a gift I was given and that I want to keep giving.

SEVEN CHAKRAS

During my yoga studies, I became fascinated with the chakras. They were so simple, yet so powerful that in India, gurus considered them "secret knowledge" too dangerous to be taught to lay people.

To me, they made so much sense.

A bright rainbow of understanding.

Simply said, they are seven spinning wheels of energy located at key points along our spine, from roots to crown. They represent life-long—and daily—journeys between the physical and the spiritual, between the Earth and the divine. They each embody physical, emotional and spiritual attributes. When one chakra is too low or too high on energy, or is blocked, our life force doesn't flow and we are out of balance. This manifests as various ailments of the body, mind and spirit.

The chakra system sees us as a whole.

It is an amazing organized map of our entire being, with seven main crossroads that need careful monitoring.

In her popular book *Wheels of Life,* Judith Anodea tells us: *More than just an assemblage of energy centers located in the body, the chakras reveal a profound mapping of universal principles, intricately nested within each other as progressively transcendent planes of reality.*

They take us on a living, throbbing journey that connects our most primal physical needs to our deepest spiritual aspirations.

The chakras help me to understand the different moods of my body and my soul.

They provide the question and the answer, wrapped into each beautiful spinning wheel.

We know where it is, therefore we know what it is, and we know what to do.

* * *

I have used the chakras to find balance in my life and help others do the same. I wish this road map was taught everywhere as a practical guide to physical and emotional wellness. I don't want anyone to wait forty years like I did to discover this treasure or, worse, never be aware it exists. Amazingly, people still believe that this ancient Vedic wisdom is New Age babble. But there's nothing new about chakras, which are looking pretty good considering they are thousands of years old!

It is very reassuring to visualize these seven wheels of energy pulsating in our bodies, reminders of our inner power, our faithful guides to physical and spiritual well-being, and our personal link to the divine.

This beautiful knowledge is meant to be shared—not as seven abstract concepts, but as seven achingly joyfully real companions.

In this book, I will utilize what I have learned to explain the chakras as I have run, strolled, marched and often stumbled on the twisting road of my life.

By telling you stories.

STORY-TELLING

Writing has always been my number one passion.

I can't draw. I can't paint. I can't sing. I can't dance. I can't even swim.

But I can write.

Words are my gift.

I am a story-teller.

So why have I always treated this precious talent as if it didn't matter, always relegating it to the back seat of my life? School, work, family, travels, friendships, service, and now yoga, have always taken precedence. I've always given them the time and devotion—without a second thought—that I would not give to the great love of my life.

When several of my childhood friends reconnected with me these past few years, their first question was: "Are you a writer now?"

After more than thirty years, this is what they remembered of me. Their most precious memories of me were my stories.

Some of my schoolmates would beg me to write more so they could read more. My younger cousins and friends remember the hours of stories I told them on our long walks. They remember the names of my characters. Names I had forgotten, like *Joe la Godasse*, hilarious member of a trio of detectives I had created.

I always had several stories running, some half-written in pencil in old, faded notebooks, still buried in my parents' attic. My imagination flowed faster than my hands, so I could never keep up with my writing. I had entire series planned out: fairy tales, mysteries, adventures, coming-of-age stories. I was so sure that I would find the time to write them all down one day. Get them published.

But I never did.

* * *

I have never stopped writing, but those were scattered moments. On a rainy day.

Or when the urge was just too strong.

I never made it a priority. As if I was afraid of abandoning myself to it. Afraid it would completely consume me and make the rest of my life irrelevant.

When I write, I don't want to stop. I don't want to eat. I don't want to talk to anyone, go anywhere. All that matters is releasing the waves of words and images that come through me onto the paper. Writing has the intensity of a passionate love affair that absorbs and devours me—a love affair with words.

We are so afraid of the music within us. So afraid of the truth of who we are. Afraid it will stir things up. Afraid it will take us away from the comfort of our lives.

And perhaps, most of all, we're afraid that we're not worthy of this truth. Our deepest fear is not that we are inadequate. Our deepest fear is that we are powerful beyond measure. It is our Light, not our Darkness, that most frightens us.

—Marianne Williamson

I feel my journey has led me where I belong: telling stories.

Carl Jung believed that every society ever created shared its knowledge through storytelling. My students often tell me how the stories I tell them in class help them to understand yoga principles that previously seemed dry and irrelevant. Making the chakras come to life with simple heartfelt stories is my gift to you, with the hope it will help you on your path.

FRANCE

I was always taught that we teach from what we know best. This is what makes us unique.

As I grow older, my French roots have become more precious to me, and my children's love and pride for their French heritage has helped me to appreciate those roots. Even after thirty-plus years with my American husband, living in an American environment, raising three American children, my "Frenchness" still colors everything I do. As I was gathering stories for this narrative, I realized that most of them related to my years in France, the place I had fought so hard to leave behind, the place that seemed the source of all my pain.

During my visits back home, I found myself asking my mother and uncles—even village neighbors—to tell me the anecdotes that used to bore and annoy me. Now I'm hungry for those little pieces of my history.

Karma's little twinkle!

* * *

With the grace of hindsight and the strength of a spiritual practice that has helped bring focus to my journey, I am ready to harmonize the music within me into a love symphony begging to be shared, meshing yogic wisdom with the humble insights I have learned on the way.

I offer you my stories with great love, hoping that my music inspires you to unveil your own symphony.

Each day for me is a musical note that I use to compose the symphony of my life.

—Paulo Coelho

ABOUT THIS BOOK

My intention is to present the chakras in a personal way anyone can relate to, intermingling real life, in all its pain and beauty, with yogic philosophy.

The mystery of yoga is not confined to the mat or scriptures; it is alive with genuine heart-pumping experiences. The best way to explain yoga is through our life testimony.

* * *

Yoga and the chakras are vibrant facets of our existence.

Their mystery continually flows into our reality.

This book is about my reality guiding you into the mystery.

Each chapter is dedicated to a chakra.

In the first part of each chapter, I take you on a journey into the stories of my life which illustrate the concept of that particular chakra. I didn't know about yoga at the time, but looking back on past events, I can see how those yogic principles were inherently part of my struggles, decisions and destiny. This ancient wisdom provides us with a map of life. I now know that this knowledge, had I been aware of it, would have helped me on my journey.

As I started each chapter, I didn't always know what aspect of that chakra would dominative my narrative and what stories would arise. I was amazed to see which memories, thought long-forgotten, naturally came up to the surface. Tears flowed with the words, tears mixed with gratitude for the lessons learned along the way.

The second part of each chapter is a definition of that chakra, how it manifests itself and how we can restore it to balance, through self-study and practical tools which have helped me personally over the years. I close each chapter with a guided meditation, written as a poetic story that allows you to creatively connect to your chakra.

At the end of the book, I give you an outline and the opportunity to share your own life journey through the chakras, with your own life stories and insight.

This book can be read as a flowing narrative, as the chapters unfold into each other. Or you can choose to focus on one chakra at a time and read each chapter individually, practicing the healing tools and doing the inner work. You can also pick one of the stories that appeals to you in one of the chapters and read it individually.

It's your road and yours alone.
Others may walk it with you, but no one can walk it for you.

—Rumi

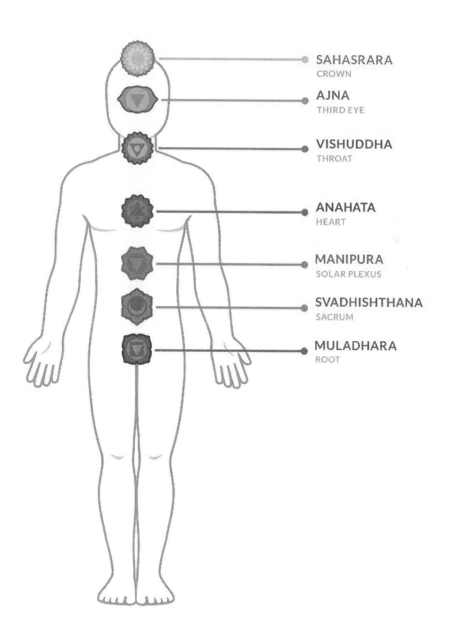

SAHASRARA
CROWN

AJNA
THIRD EYE

VISHUDDHA
THROAT

ANAHATA
HEART

MANIPURA
SOLAR PLEXUS

SVADHISHTHANA
SACRUM

MULADHARA
ROOT

CHAPTER 1

MULADHARA
ROOT CHAKRA

Treasure your roots even if they're weeds

Maybe you are searching among the branches for what only appears in the roots.

—Rumi

Muladhara is our root system, everything that makes us feel safe, grounded and stable. It is the primal foundation of our life journey, where everything begins. It is our tribe, our family history, our link to our ancestors, our cultural essence and identity.

It is often the chakra we take for granted, the part of ourselves we leave behind with no intention of ever looking back, especially if we have a painful past. Of course, we know we have roots. We tell ourselves that the reason why no one can see the roots of trees and plants is that they are supposed to stay hidden. Out of sight, out of mind! We are much more interested in growing branches, something that can be seen and admired.

Muladhara is buried at the base of our being. We might think that it is meant to be forgotten, but we fail to remember that our roots are not only where everything started but that without them, nothing can continue. If we don't nurture and take care of a plant's roots, the plant will stop growing. If we ignore the sickness of those roots, it will spread to the whole plant, to our whole life. Without a healthy root system, we will never grow. Without that foundation, our spirit will not thrive.

The biggest mistake we can make is to neglect our roots. Without them there is no journey, no music. Muladhara is the first note of our symphony, it is the paper on which it is written, the chair we sit on and the pen in our hand. It is the essential and steadfast foundation of every meaningful journey.

It took me a long time to learn that lesson.

THE PESKY DANDELIONS

What is a weed? A plant whose virtues have not been discovered.
—Ralph Waldo Emerson

When I was home in France for a short visit, spring was in its early stages. I noticed bright touches of yellow in places where I rarely see them in my American environment. Don't get me wrong: spring in Virginia is magnificent, alive with burning reds and pinks of azalea bushes, delicate lacy whites of dogwood, velvety frilly pink canopies of cherry trees, cheery bluebells and friendly yellow clumps of daffodils. But those are usually neatly positioned in flower beds, borders and on roadsides.

No, back in my childhood village, the yellow touches were random, wild, undisciplined. In one word: unwanted.

Indeed, these were carpets of dandelions scattered on every lawn, front and back of every house. As we sipped apéritif on their verandah, all the friends I visited lamented the horror of those pests that ruined their grass. They went on and on about the plight of the *salopris de pissenlis*—the dreadful dandelion—while I secretly marveled at how amazingly beautiful this bright yellow on dark green looked. My friends dreamed of perfect American lawns while I envied their carefree colorful meadows of weeds. They told me horror stories of hours spent on hands and knees trying to pull out those pesky roots, one at a time, to no avail. Their roots were so strong, so tough. You could pull them, but they always came back. What was there to do?

"Why don't you just let them be?" I ventured. "They're beautiful!" Incredulous looks and answers: "But they're weeds!"

"Who says they are?"

"They just are, because they grow everywhere and you can't get rid of them!"

"What's wrong about that if they're beautiful?"

I thought for so long that my roots were weeds, because of the pain and the struggles within me that grew where they were unwanted.

I thought that I could just pull them and I would get rid of all my unpleasant memories. I had created a beautiful life, and I thought for so long that this was because I had pulled all those roots.

I was wrong.

My life was meaningful because I had never successfully pulled my roots; they ran too deep. The beauty in my life had grown from those unwanted roots which had given it its texture and color. They had never given up, even if I had. They knew I would come back and open my eyes to their relevance.

We cannot escape our roots; they are too strong, too tough, and too deep.

Trying to pull them out just hurts us.

We don't really know what they'll grow into, and isn't it just a matter of perspective?

Is a dandelion ugly or beautiful?

Is it a weed or a flower?

SHELTERS

The ache for home lives in all of us, the safe place where we can go as we are and not be questioned.

—Maya Angelou

When I think of my early years, I think of my maternal grandparents: Mémé and Pépé.

Thinking of them makes me feel warm and safe. They have influenced me more than they could have ever known, giving me the simple foundations on which I built my life.

My parents were very busy, and I spent most of my time in my grandparents' small kitchen, sitting and reading by the shiny wood stove in winter and, in summer, on the windowsill overlooking the giant plane tree in the front yard. This was the ultimate safe place for me, where the world started and ended, where I mapped out the great adventures of my future. My early years were cradled in the comforting aromatic rhythms of the seasons: fall mushroom omelets and wild partridges or pheasants, caught by my uncles, roasted in herbs and butter, hearty winter vegetable soups simmering on the stove, spring's first salads tossed with fresh garlic and sharp mustard vinaigrette and summer's bounty of luscious fruits—strawberries, blackberries, raspberries, red currants, black currants and apricots—ripe with juice and sweetness, cooked for hours inside a huge tall pot into fragrant mouth-watering jams and jellies that would lend to the other seasons a taste of summer.

Mémé and Pépé were the buttresses of my world, always there, arms open, happy to see me. They were the ones I rushed to when I had good news. They were the ones who loved me without demands. I realize now how I must have taken them for granted, their presence a matter of fact in the grand scheme of my life, clueless that their invaluable simplicity was a virtue that would shape the person I am today.

* * *

Francine and Albert were born in 1914, at the onset of World War I, and had grown up during the lean years following that calamitous period. Then, their love story, union and fledgling family were caught in the horrors of World War II, with the actual invasion of their country and their village. Five years of their lives were dominated by the stomping of heavy German boots. They were afraid of what might happen next, busy scavenging enough ration stamps for their family, struggling to survive. They rarely talked about it, but the stories were all around me: the acts of bravery of the Resistance, the assistance to American and English soldiers, the ruthless German retaliations, always engulfed in constant fear. I could not imagine such horrors, so I heard those tales with detachment. The fact that I learned it in school also made it all so distant, so passé.

My grandmother's life revolved around her daily chores: working in the garden, picking up vegetables for lunch and dinner, cooking, cleaning and taking care of her church. Her love for the *Sainte Vierge* was all encompassing and she reserved her best flowers for her statue.

Mémé's only indulgences were her sacrosanct nap after lunch, the occasional afternoon coffee and gossip with ladies from the village or with one of her six children. She listened to them tell their stories and relished their triumphs as if they were her own. She had a purity of heart that is rare today in our over-stimulated, media-saturated society, because the seat of her soul was never distracted by the outside. She never watched television, rarely listened to the radio and only read the newspaper when her family was mentioned in it. Her code of ethics was ruled by the Catholic Church which clearly narrowed her world, but she needed the safety and reassurance of those restrictions.

Years of deprivation had left Mémé content with the comfort and modesty of her routines and with a fear of anything that took her away from them. But hardship had given Pépé a shameless lust for life and a total disregard for public opinion. He was gregarious; his simplicity lay in his zest for life. He was the most resourceful person I knew and he could be very cunning. He was a self-taught man raised in foster homes who had managed to find his way into the ramifications of French social networking. He was retired from the SNCF (Société Nationale des Chemins de Fer)—railroad—and he volunteered for several charitable organizations. This leisure time gave him the opportunity to travel around France and, as I heard my relatives whisper, to cheat on my grandmother. I didn't believe them. They had separate bedrooms, but I assumed this was because they were too old to sleep together. They argued a lot and Mémé pulled away when he tried to kiss her. This was what I was used to.

People loved him or hated him. He could be violent and have terrible fits, but they never lasted long. He was also Catholic, but on his own terms, and he made no excuses.

Their relationship was imperfect and highly dysfunctional. They co-existed from the force of habit, but probably would not have wanted it any other way. Their generation did not believe that they were owed a "fairy tale" life; they accepted the hand they had been dealt with grace and courage. Having survived the war without losing anyone, having food on the table and money in the bank was recognized for the blessing that it was. When one has survived so much chaos, life is a gift. They each handled their gift in a different way.

I loved them both: my Mémé's naiveté and my Pépé's bravado.

I liked that they were so different, because I recognized myself in both of them.

I know now that I am both of them.

* * *

In the early seventies, when I was eleven, Pépé renovated the "big room" downstairs. It was called *salle du catéchisme* because it had been used by the village priest to teach catechism before my grandparents owned the house. Pépé divided it into a bathroom and a small living-room. Mémé was furious; she loved the big room where our whole family gathered for celebrations. She raged and tried to stop him, but he was adamant. He wanted a television and he needed a room in which to watch it. He bought the first color television set in the whole village.

Mémé never used either of those rooms. She continued living upstairs in her kitchen and adjoining bedroom, and washed herself at the kitchen sink until the end of her days.

I loved Pépé's new room. It had a comfortable leather couch under the big windows, a side table and a round table in the middle. In the beginning, everyone came to watch the soccer and rugby games in color.

The novelty wore off when people purchased their own color televisions.

A strange new pattern started to emerge. My visits to my grandparents had always brought me to the kitchen, Mémé's domain. I would see Pépé when he came upstairs, which never made Mémé happy, or outside in the front yard or in one of his gardens.

My grandmother was everyone's favorite, but I loved my grandfather just as much. Now that he had his own room, I would stop downstairs to spend time with him before or after visiting Mémé in the kitchen. I would also relay messages from one to the other, climbing up the steep stairs several times during each visit. It might seem like a bizarre upstairs-downstairs arrangement, but it felt perfectly normal to me. They were different and needed their own separate space. And I liked visiting them separately; they could not be together more than a few minutes without starting a chain of arguments and bickering that sickened me. This way, I got the best of both of them.

Depending upon how I felt, I spent more time in one room than the other.

Upstairs when I needed comfort and reassurance.

Downstairs when I needed support for my most daring dreams and real life issues.

Mémé rescued me from myself.

Pépé rescued me from the world's harshness.

They were my two shelters.

SURVIVAL

We shall draw from the heart of suffering itself the means of inspiration and survival.

—Winston Churchill

I needed shelters because life at home was not always easy.
My father was not an easy man.

I heard him described that way countless times: *"Il n'est pas facile!"*

He was so unpredictable that I remember wishing him gone many times—not forever, but gone for the day, the week.

Just gone so we could breathe.

Life was easier when he was gone. We didn't have to walk on egg shells and worry about what mood he would be in.

He was a trained carpenter but chose to work as a truck driver because he didn't want to be around people. Sometimes he had to work nights. Those night shift weeks were a nightmare for all of us. He got up at midnight, so he went to bed early and could not tolerate any noise. If he thought we—or the television—were too loud, he would come out of his bedroom, scream, slam doors and unplug the television. He behaved the same way in the afternoon when he came home from work and took his long nap after lunch. We had to be quiet until he got up.

Our lives revolved around his schedule.

He wanted a simple life: work, gardening, regular meals and some television. His only passion was rugby and, perhaps, his garden.

My father and my mother had a tormented relationship. They fought often. He never abused her physically but his words were cruel, doors were slammed and things were broken.

Spirits were broken too.

I hated the way he made her cry, how their fights affected my younger brother Patrice and me, how alone we felt when they fought. Maman would lock herself in the attic for hours—sometimes days—telling me that she wanted to die and that I needed to take care of my brother. I did not know who to turn to. I was too ashamed and too scared to tell anyone.

Yet, Papa was the epitome of what we call in French *un homme droit,* literally translated as a straight man: an honest, decent man. This is one of the highest compliments you can give a person in France.

He was not religious—he described church-going people as hypocrites—but he had strong ethics. He despised liars and cheaters.

Papa was also strangely prudish, and could not stand it when my uncles told dirty jokes during family dinners.

He was a man of moderation, the least greedy person I have ever known. He enjoyed good food but never over-ate. He was the one who taught me that one square of dark chocolate with coffee after lunch is just enough to satisfy.

He was not vain and he lacked any kind of ambition, which caused some of the friction with Maman. He only read rugby and gardening magazines. Despite that, his words sometimes had the kind of insight that startled me and made me realize he was so much more than what he allowed us to see. He was highly intelligent, but hid it well.

My father was a secret that I only started to understand when it was too late.

As a child, you take your parents as they are; you don't think that they have a history, you don't think of unraveling all the layers of their psyche. You think of them as the guiding lights of your world.

But how can they guide you when they are so lost themselves?

I didn't want a complicated father, a father whose behavior confused and angered me. I just wanted a normal father who would guide me and my brother.

He was not a normal father.

So, I gave up on him.

It has taken me many years to finally understand why he was the way he was. I wish I could tell him that now.

I know now why his routine was so vital to him and why he could not stand anything that disturbed it.

It was his lifeline.

It kept him from feeling.

It was his only way to survive the trauma of his childhood.

* * *

Papa was born in 1933 on Bastille Day in Vienne, France, the third of five children.

When he was six, France was occupied by the Germans.

When he was seven, his father Leonard hanged himself in an outbuilding. Papa and his brother René found him.

The occupying German forces requisitioned what they wanted, including Léonard's business. From one day to the next, this proud man had no way to provide for his family. He also had tuberculosis. He feared he would infect his loved ones, especially his newborn son, and he took his own life to save them.

After his death, his young widow Louise could not feed all her children. Her new baby would, sadly, not survive and would die of tuberculosis. So, she sent her strongest child, my father, *petit Marcel*, to live with Léonard's sister and her husband, Léa and Kiki, on their farm in the majestic Vercors mountains.

I believe her intentions were pure and kind. Marcel would have plenty to eat there and she believed he would heal the hearts of his aunt and uncle.

Papa was entering the third drama of his young life.

Léa and Kiki's only child—a ten-year old daughter—had recently died of appendicitis. A very simple operation would have saved her, but the local doctor had been sent to the front and had never come back.

Papa—his small shoulders already burdened with too much pain— arrived in a home that lived to the rhythm of more pain. Léa and Kiki were good, decent people, but they were irremediably heartbroken, living their lives to the slow, deliberate pace of grief.

They cared for that intense, dark-haired, dark-eyed little boy, but he could not replace their little girl.

They had hardened. They were afraid to love again.

Kiki was an active member of the *Résistance*, devoting his life to the fight against those invaders whose presence had killed his little girl. Léa moved through life in a daze, letting herself go and losing herself in hard work.

Marcel had plenty to eat on the farm, but lived a life of no frills; there were no Christmases, no birthdays, no hugs, no bedtime kisses or stories, no open affection.

In just a few months, he had lost his father, his mother and his siblings—whom he rarely saw afterwards—and his childhood.

He most certainly had what now has a name—PTSD—and he carried it with him all his life.

And he carried us alongside it: Maman, Patrice and me.

Papa loved his aunt and uncle, and respected them greatly for raising him. They were an important part of our lives until they died.

But he never forgave his mother for "abandoning" him, as well as his siblings whom she had kept with her.

He told me once that he did not have a mother.

* * *

Papa met Maman—Thérèse—while he was doing his one-year compulsory military service on the Army base where she worked. She was eighteen and he was twenty. She tells the story often: "All the girls in the office were talking about the new guy and how good-looking he was. I fell for him as soon as I saw him. He had that dark brooding look, his curly black hair slicked back and his gaze penetrating. He also had a motorcycle, hence the cool factor. I would spy on him through the window, but pretended to ignore him when he came into my office. One time, he stole my scarf and I yelled at him. He said he would give it back only if I went to the cinema with him."

They waited two years to get married because they had no money. Papa went back home to live with his aunt and uncle, to work and to save. They wrote to each other and he would ride his motorcycle sixty miles to come and see her whenever he could. "He loved me so much, we had a wonderful courtship. I knew he had had a rough childhood and I wanted to take care of him, make him happy. But he changed after we married; he had this dark side that would just appear out of nowhere."

* * *

Papa was a man of sharp contrasts.

He was not afraid to tell people exactly what he thought—sometimes in the most abrupt way—yet everyone respected him.

He treated Maman with cruelty, yet he was extremely proud of her and was lost without her. He was her most ruthless critic and her strongest defender.

He was the most unsociable person I knew, yet he could be the most charming man in the whole room. Women were undoubtedly attracted to him, which left me baffled, because I knew my ideal man was his total opposite.

He was not active in my brother's life nor in mine, but he was extremely proud of us. He often told me that he had complete trust in me and my decisions, and I took it as a poor excuse for his indifference. I didn't understand at the time that this was the highest compliment he could give me.

* * *

During one of his unwarranted screaming fits, I screamed back at him: "I hate you and how miserable you make us all feel!" I added that my only wish was to leave and move as far away from him as I could, and to never see him again.

I'll never forget the tortured way he looked at me.

Unknowingly, I had touched the core of his misery: abandonment.

He became very calm and told me: "I know very well that you're going to leave and never come back. Go ahead, even though it's going to shatter me."

Of course, I came back, with my husband, our children, hoping to share some of the joys of my new life with him and Maman.

He still carried his burden, but I know he had some happy moments with us during our visits, and with Maman too, when they started taking annual vacations to Provence.

But, unfortunately, grief was not done with him.

His last years on earth were even more painful than his early years: my brother died of cancer and Papa had a stroke that left him crippled on his left side. Ten years later, he died, early and excruciatingly, of colon cancer.

He welcomed death.

* * *

The bright light is that, during his last lucid days, he and Maman had a chance to talk. Really talk. He told her how much he had always loved her, and he apologized for the way he had treated her. He said he could not help it; those moments of intense rage would just overpower him. He had always been faithful to her, even though—Maman likes to add—he had plenty of opportunities.

He thanked her for giving him children, and said our births were the happiest moments of his life. He was so proud to build a family with her.

A family he never had.

When she asked him, he could not explain to her why he acted as if he wanted to destroy what he cherished the most.

I understand now that it was simply an act of survival, carried over by a seven-year-old little boy.

My mother tells me often that I am just like my father.

It used to be a veiled reproach when she was cross with me, but now, it's a compliment.

It means I am a decent, honest person.

LAVENDER ICE-CREAM

All things must come to the soul from its roots, from where it is planted.

—Saint Teresa of Avila

There was a time when all I could see were weeds in my past.

Now I can see bright, gorgeous, yellow flowers.

They are still the same dandelions.

But I can see more clearly now. As Marcel Proust wrote: *The real voyage of discovery consists not in seeking new landscapes but in having new eyes.*

For a while, all I seemed to remember were the undercurrents of pain in my family that I did not understand, the endless fighting of my parents and grandparents, and what I perceived as the indifference of the rest of my family, the stuffiness of what I thought was their suffocating world.

All I wanted was to create new memories, in new places, with new languages, new people and my new family.

I did that.

But I kept coming back.

To share my happiness.

But nothing seemed to change.

I kept taking in their pain.

Then tragedy arrived.

One after the other, all the people I loved died.

My grandmother, my brother, my grandfather, my father...

Every visit to France was a visit to pain.

The five stages of grieving, repeated over and over again: denial, anger, bargaining, depression. But never acceptance.

I could not even stand my country any longer. I loathed everything French. French to me was the synonym for pain, oppressive, heart-clenching pain.

When the plane would land in Lyon's airport, Saint-Exupéry, my stomach would tighten, just like my breath.

People would tell me how lucky I was to be French, how much they loved France, how beautiful it was. I did not remember any beauty. All I remembered was grief.

Until I could not stand it any longer and I took a break from my roots, from my family. After Papa died.

* * *

I came back to France on my own the year following his death. I had to see it with new eyes, without visiting my relatives. I reacquainted myself with my country, with my heritage, on my own terms.

I ambled through flea markets and old bookstores, strolled the streets of my favorite cities, visited friends I never had time to visit, learned how to make crêpes in a real crêperie, read *Tintin* and *Astérix* books, took the train, rode the bus, wore pretty sundresses in the markets and promenades of Provence and Côte d'Azur, sipped black espresso on the terrace of cafés, walked the streets of Paris with my two young sons, got lost in the *traboules* of *Vieux Saint-Jean* in Old Lyon, and ate ice-cream that tasted like flowers: lilac, rose, violet, poppy, lavender.

This is when I realized that any place that has ice-cream that tastes like flowers is pretty special.

I am a product of this place.

A dandelion.

A survivor.

Still growing wild and strong, just like my ancestors.

I am proud of my roots.

As Buddha said, *not letting them be a burden, but a joy!*

1. THE ROOT CHAKRA: MULADHARA

COLOR: Red
SANSKRIT TRANSLATION: Root Support
KEY WORDS: Tribe, Family, Survival Instinct, Security
LOCATION: Base of spine

RELATED BODY PARTS:
Skeleton, Joints, Teeth, Legs and Feet, Bladder, Elimination System, Lymph System

QUALITIES WHEN BALANCED:
Feeling Safe and Grounded, Fearlessness, Abundance, Sense of Belonging, At Home in your Body

PSYCHOLOGICAL SIGNS OF IMBALANCE:
Instability, Stress, Phobia and Anxiety, Anger, Fear Related to Survival and Abandonment, Disconnection, Scarcity Consciousness, Financial Problems

PHYSICAL SIGNS OF IMBALANCE:
Problems with Feet, Legs, Bones and Joints, Arthritis, Sciatica, Weight Issues, Hemorrhoids, Constipation

POSITIVE ARCHETYPE: The Earth Mother/Father
NEGATIVE ARCHETYPE: The Victim
ELEMENT: Earth
SENSE: Smell
SOUND: LAM
VERB: I Am Here
FOOD: Proteins

HEALING TOOLS

Self-study:

- Do you have any dandelions in your life?

- What were your shelters growing up?

- What does survival mean to you?

- Do you have anyone in your life who lives/lived in survival mode like my father?

- What is your lavender ice-cream? What makes your history/ your heritage special?

- What makes you feel unsafe and afraid?

- What makes you feel safe and grounded?

Practical tools:

- Write down your feelings of fears and insecurities and consciously let them go, replacing them with what makes you feel safe. You can burn them in a little ceremony
- Reconnect with your family history by looking at old pictures or talking with a relative or a member of your cultural community
- Study your family heritage
- Learn and read about your homeland, the country of your ancestors
- Wear red, place red flowers, a bowl of red fruit or red decorative items in your home
- Meditate for at least three minutes at dawn and dusk, when day and night meet
- Do a walking meditation barefoot in dirt, grass, sand or mud
- Stand barefoot in dirt, grass, sand or mud
- Connect to Nature: sit against a tree, work in your garden, put your hands in soil
- Research Native American rituals and practice the ones that appeal to you
- Enjoy a foot massage
- Take a mud bath

ASANAS: Standing: Tadasana and Temple; Balancing: Tree, Dancer, Eagle, Warrior I and II; Goddess, Squat

MANTRA: *I am Safe and Grounded*

ROOT CHAKRA MEDITATION

Find a comfortable place where you feel safe and grounded
Sitting or lying down
Relaxing into the body and into the breath
Taking a deep breath in and a long breath out
Sending the breath to the base of your spine
Feeling the breath as a beautiful red glow that nourishes and warms the
 base of your spine
Repeating your Mantra: *I am Safe and Grounded*
Starting to visualize yourself walking with bare feet through a field of
 freshly turned earth
Feeling the way each step grounds you into the earth
The warm soft red soil
With its intoxicating fragrance
And the way it molds itself around your bare feet
I am Safe and Grounded
Suddenly feeling a rain drop on your cheek
Another one
And another
Starting to run, bare feet slapping the red earth
Desperately looking for shelter
Seeing it
Standing in the middle of the field
A majestic red maple tree in all its autumn glory
A burst of hope
A safe place
Finding refuge under its red canopy
And hugging its regal trunk, pressing your whole body against it
I am Safe and Grounded
As the rain intensifies, its branches seem to open into a splendid red
 umbrella
Not one single rain drop passes through

I am Safe and Grounded

Sitting against the tree, your back resting against its strong trunk

Protected as the rain keeps falling

Relaxing and smiling, safely snuggled against the sturdiness of the red
tree

Both of you firmly grounded into the red earth

As its roots become your roots

And its presence becomes your presence

You have found your shelter

I am Safe and Grounded.

CHAPTER 2

SVADHISHTHANA
SACRAL CHAKRA

Some relationships are forever, some are for a season

No love, no friendship can cross the path of our destiny without leaving some mark on it.

—François Mauriac

After we have established our roots, chakra philosophy tells us that we go out and expand our circle of relationships, looking for buddies, mates, men and women with whom we can share our lives.

In order to grow, we open ourselves to the outside world. Venturing outside of the safety of our tribe, where all is pre-ordained, brings with it the frightening concept of choice and change.

As we mature into Svadhishthana, we learn this most amazing human paradigm: the ability to create our own story. In this process, we meet and choose the people who will be part of that story. With every great gift, comes great fear and responsibility, and the intoxicating power of choice can either enrich or diminish our essence. The allure of power, sex and money—the main players in many human relationships—can have a negative, addictive hold on us. Human interactions can also be fraught with pain and disappointment when the other person doesn't treat us as we wish to be treated or when life separates us. But if we tread carefully and accept that change is an integral part of human connections, we will be able to use those human desires and aches as positive creative assets to enrich our lives and those of others.

It is another step in our growth, taking us out of our initial comfort zone, allowing us to spread our emotional wings into new territories.

We could say that we are building a family of choice. We did not choose our original family, but we are choosing our friends, partners and spouses. We want to find the special people who will accompany us on our journey. Some of them will stay with us, but we have to accept that many of them will only be our traveling companions for a short while. And perhaps—such is the beauty of life—our roads will cross again.

THE PAINS OF CHANGE AND GROWING UP

To exist is to change, to change is to mature, to mature is to go on creating oneself endlessly.

—Henri Bergson

Some of us stay pretty close to our tribe. A great majority of the youth who grew up with me dated and married others from their village or neighboring towns.

They were the epitome of normal to me at the time, that normal I could not seem to grasp. I had realized in my early teens that I just didn't live and breathe to the same tempo as everyone around me. I always felt out of sync, lacking the rhythm of my surroundings. And, to a family and a limited social circle firmly entrenched in the normal, especially as appearances went, this was a big no-no.

Everything seemed to predestine me to be different. I always went to different schools than the young people around me. My parents were not wealthy but, as a young girl, Maman always promised herself that she would send her daughter to the private boarding school her parents could not afford. From preschool to college, I attended establishments that sounded like a Catholic litany of saints: Jeanne d'Arc, Sainte Marie and Sacré-Coeur.

People branded me as "shy and studious," which at the time was more or less a label for "unsociable and nerdy." At eleven, an age when circles of friends become important, we moved from our larger town, Lagnieu, to my grandparents' small village, Leyment. It was only five miles away but, at a time when we had no close public transportation and no phone (phone lines in our region only reached every household in 1976 when I was fifteen), I may as well have lived in the middle of a desert.

I lived in a small world, where there were few people to choose from, no room for errors and not many lifestyle choices. Once you were put in a box, you stayed in it. You belonged or you did not.

Those circumstances emphasized my introversion. I always felt separate from everyone's story, from the children of the village who all shared years of school together, from the children in my private schools who lived in different towns and had their own lives there, and from my own relatives who were either too old or too young.

With the reassuring blessing of hindsight, I realize that this was just the way it was supposed to be and I am grateful that I did not try to force myself into a pulse of life that did not match the way I felt, but shortened my breath and breadth of life.

It certainly didn't feel good at the time. We all want to belong, to match the pattern of our world. We all crave acceptance and approval. Going against the grain grates and chafes, doesn't make one popular, makes others uncomfortable and, consequently, often the butt of jokes and ridicule. A difficult experience, especially in one's tender youth.

Throughout this journey, I think that my greatest quality—and my greatest weakness—was to give myself to all relationships with über sincerity, eagerness and trust. When you feel different, and finally meet someone who seems to understand and like you, it's such a relief that you dive right into it with reckless abandonment.

Consequently, the friendships I developed were precious. When I finally found someone who seemed to think like me, I was totally invested. And when it ended, I was often devastated.

CHILDHOOD'S FRIEND

Each friend represents a world in us, a world not born until they arrive, and it is only by this meeting that a new world is born.
—Anais Nin

My first best friend, Catherine, was also my very first friend. We went to school together from kindergarten through high school. We were both at the top of our classes and, even though we didn't openly talk about it, we were always competing for first place. This innocent rivalry invigorated us because we both had an incredible thirst for learning.

We took piano lessons from the same teacher, an obese old maid from an impoverished noble family who lived in a cluttered small apartment in Lagnieu, smelled rank, had mood swings and hit our fingers with a ruler when she was in a bad mood.

Catherine and I both loved literature and English, dreaming of trips to England. We were avid readers, exchanging *Club des Cinq* (*Famous Five*) books by Enid Blyton, and Nancy Drew (called *Alice* in the French translations), before moving on to Verlaine and Baudelaire poetry, Victor Hugo, Guy de Maupassant, Jean Giono and Boris Vian.

We both loved music, but Catherine truly was the expert. She introduced me to the Beatles, the Rolling Stones and The Who. I loved the Osmonds, until she told me they were lame. We would spend entire afternoons in her basement figuring out the lyrics of *Let it be* or *The fool on the hill*, creating dance routines, imagining that we were famous rock stars.

My true love was writing and we would write together, read each other's stories, compose poetry *à quatre mains* (with four hands) in our boarding school's study hall.

Even though we were linked together as the true example of two best friends, we were inherently very different. Those differences helped us grow and create our distinct personalities but, as we matured into our uncomfortable teenage years, those divergences became more obvious and harder to ignore. Catherine was very social and wanted to fit into the popular crowd. I was socially inept—an odd mixture of shyness and fearlessness—and fitting in was not my priority. Also, our families were utterly different: Catherine's parents seemed to have a stable relationship and her mother was always available to pick me up and drive me home from our play dates. They went on annual summer vacations. On the other hand, my parents both worked and Maman was an active volunteer. She was always busy. We never went on family vacations and my parents' fights were frequent and violent. I was too ashamed to share this with anyone, including Catherine. My worst fear was to appear weak and lacking, so I acted like everything was fine.

We drifted apart in high school. We tried to drag each other along like tattered old toys that we kept by force of habit. But it was no use. Our "best friend" status had reached its expiration date and we were ready to go our own way.

Catherine and I reconnected twenty years later after my father died. We had gone through all the stages of adulthood we used to fantasize about: college, jobs, marriage and children. After all this time, it felt comfortable to naturally fall back into the familiar themes of our teenage conversations, now sprinkled with the insight of maturity and experience. We both still loved books, movies and languages and shared a strong political affinity and sense of social justice.

I do believe that some friendships are meant to bookend our lives, with a necessary separation in the middle. We grow up together but we have to continue the adult part of our journey by ourselves. If we try too hard to fit into those friendships and be the friend they want us to be, we will just be a follower, and will regret it later. Letting go can be painful but also liberating. It is the only way we can become who we are supposed to be. And reuniting with someone who knew us at the beginning of our journey allows us to see how much we have grown.

It is a blessing to share our life with old friends. Again.

THE SHORT INTENSE FRIENDSHIP

When you part from your friend, you grieve not; For that which you love most in him may be clearer in his absence, as the mountain to the climber is clearer from the plain.

—Kahlil Gibran

Some friendships die without any explanation.

Samuel was my intellectual Jewish soul buddy in high school. I spent hours discussing philosophy and the meaning of life with him. He was probably the first friend who really challenged my intellect. The first friend who really "got me."

We shared a desk in the back of study hall (seats were assigned for the year) during 11th grade, and those two hours every evening before dinner were probably my fondest high school moments.

We wrote each other letters during our school breaks. He was the only person I told about my parents' constant fighting. He told me that this was not my problem, that I needed to live my own life and that I could not fix them. I could not fix anyone. This was probably the best advice anyone ever gave me.

He was truthful and relentless and I fell in love with the duels of our minds, and probably with him.

He was quirky and awkward but he made me feel alive. Unfortunately, as the only child of older high-achieving parents, he had a chip on his shoulder: mediocre grades which he constantly compared to my good grades. In the middle of 12th grade, he started to resent me. Then, almost as if to spite me, he asked a mutual friend out on a date.

When I tried to talk to him, he told me I was arrogant, righteous and not living in the real world. He said that I had all those dreams that were unreal and that I needed to fit in instead of living in an imaginary world.

I did not understand: we had both taken so much pleasure in discussing all those lofty philosophical ideas. This had been our common link, but he was now breaking it. I felt betrayed to my core. I wrote him a long angry letter, unknowingly justifying what he had told me. I was arrogant, judgmental and righteous.

He did not answer; he never talked to me again.

I had not realized how important this short friendship had been to me until I started this chapter. I had forgotten Samuel, but he flowed onto the paper out of nowhere. Even though our relationship ended so abruptly, he had made high school bearable and, for a short while, had given me a safe place to be *me*. He made me realize it was okay to be different.

He also taught me a lesson I was not ready to learn: humility.

I should have heeded his advice: you cannot change anyone.

MY ROCK

Love one another, but make not a bond of love:
Let it rather be a moving sea between the shores of your souls.
—Kahlil Gibran

During my dating years in my twenties, I remember vividly what one of my more experienced "guy friends" told me when I asked him; "How do you know when you meet the right person?"

"You'll know because everything will feel so natural. You won't worry about him calling you or you calling him. He will be there for you. Unconditionally."

I remembered those words when I met my future husband, John, in Frankfurt, Germany a few months later. Friendship and love flowed naturally. Effortlessly. We just knew that it was meant to be.

John wrote once in a college essay that I was the anchor to his balloon, that he had been floating aimlessly until he met me. He said I gave him a sense of direction, a purpose.

To me, he is my rock, my safe place.

I've always been an explorer, a seeker. I am passionate in my convictions and often impulsive in my reactions. I believe in fairness, freedom and equality for all but I'm not always tactful in my search for justice. I ride on the wings of myriad ideas and dreams. I go on quests, out at sea even when I can't swim, out in the wilderness even when I'm terrified. He is the rock that I can hang on to when I lose breath or hope, the rock I can safely land on when I need a refuge before my next adventure. He is my Skellig Michael rising out of the mist after an endless stormy boat ride on the Atlantic.

Marriage/partnership is not about having a smooth ride. It is more of a white-water rafting experience. It is about swaying with the current of life while being a rock or an anchor for each other. Sometimes I want to kick that rock, and I'm sure he wants to kick that anchor. But without my rock, I would get lost when I fly high, when I lose track of time and reality.

From this rock, I can move freely and creatively in the world.

My rock helps me to build castles.

MOTHERHOOD

You have within you more love that you could ever understand.
—Rumi

I just turned fifty-five and my daughter turned thirty.

When she was born, I was almost twenty-five and my path suddenly seemed so clear. After years of searching for love and meaning, I thought I finally had it all figured out.

The priorities set during my innocent childhood and my awkward teenage years had totally changed. I never thought that being a mother was part of my destiny. I didn't think there would be time. I didn't think there would be anyone to share my life. I was on a one-person track to gather success and experiences. Looking back, I see that my journey until then had been about proving a point, most of all to myself. I thought proving that point was my purpose.

It was, in a way, because those experiences had brought me to that moment when the German nurse brought me this tiny wrinkled creature wrapped in a blanket and uttered those magic words I never thought I would hear: *"Mutti, hier kommt deine Tochter."*

My daughter, France-Lee.

As I leaned back against the pillows of my hospital bed, holding this precious new life John and I had created, the big, warm cocoon of motherhood, the most primal sense of relevance since the beginning of time, wrapped me into its warm embrace and made everything else unimportant. This maternal certainty has been growing and coloring my life ever since with the vibrancy of unconditional love. I needed it to become who I am today.

Almost six years later, in the heat of Panama, our little boy JC came into our lives, followed by his brother Patou two years later.

Being a mother had never been part of my dreams and expectations.

But it was meant to be my journey.

Being a lonely child mostly preoccupied with taking care of myself, motherhood painstakingly taught me to give without expecting anything in return, to protect and guide even if it makes me "the bad guy" at the time. It taught me to be humble and to get off my pedestal. It taught me to be me.

My children have helped me become someone I never thought I would be.

THE ANGELS

Friendship is the purest love… where nothing is asked for, no condition, where one simply enjoys giving.

—Osho

When John and I moved from Germany to New Jersey with our two-year old little girl, we were starting from scratch. We barely had any furniture and had left all our friends behind. I also was a brand new American military wife and didn't know any of the unwritten rules of that role that was so foreign to me.

Two weeks after we arrived, John came to the guest-house where we were staying with a dinner invitation from the wife of one of his co-workers. When I met Jean, I met someone who walked the talk, someone who helped without condescension or expectation. I soon realized that this short robust little woman, ten years my senior, dressed in baggy sweat shirts and Mom jeans was a powerful force on our military post. She was the head of the volunteer program. She helped because it was her nature. She upset some of the high-ranking officers' wives who thought of service on Fort Monmouth as their prerogative and resented this simple enlisted spouse making such a big impact. But Jean didn't play those games. She didn't inspire admiration because of her husband's position or a perfectly decorated house on officer's row, fancy clothes and parties. She inspired because she was real. Her house was modest and cluttered, her dinners were unpretentious, Christmas with her family was rowdy and fun and she didn't need to impress.

She welcomed us into her home, introduced me to her network of friends and explained the intricacies of military life. She helped me without making a big deal out of it. She found us furniture: a bed, dressers and a dining set. I joined her in her volunteer work. When I asked her how I could repay her for her kindness, she said: "I don't want anything back. My best reward is for you to help someone when you're able."

I have met many other angels like Jean, such as Shari, another military spouse, who supported me after my brother's death and hosted a surprise baby shower for my third baby in Panama when she heard that I had never had a shower before. Or the friend in Munich who let me sleep on the floor of her tiny rented bedroom for several weeks when I left an abusive situation with my German host family. Those are the people who show us through their selfless actions what true goodness is. They don't have any expectations. They are just authentic generous people who inspire us to do the same for others.

This is the kind of friend I aspire to be.

Let no one ever come to you without leaving happier.

—Mother Teresa

SOUL BUDDIES

When two people relate to each other authentically and humanly, God is the electricity that surges between them.

—Martin Buber

One of the most extraordinary feelings in the universe is to recognize someone's soul as clearly as our own. We all yearn for those encounters that go right to the center of our being, bypassing the polite ritual of small talk. You might meet those soul buddies in a crowded airplane, as I once did on an eight-hour transatlantic flight from Amsterdam to Philadelphia with a Dutchman whose name I don't remember. Our conversation had the intensity of a love affair, as we dug relentlessly into the depths of our most secret beliefs and dreams, in three different languages, and left each other satiated but still longing for all the words that had been left unsaid.

I know for a fact that those encounters become more frequent once we find our way. We know we're on the right path when we start meeting more fellow soul travelers. For me, one of the greatest blessings of finding and teaching yoga has been encountering many "soul buddies" who have become my dearest friends. I don't know all the details of their lives, but I recognize the longings of their souls. Yoga makes it possible to reveal who we truly are in a non-apologetic way. We meet others who breathe and vibrate to the same frequency as we do and we become each other's support system. It's okay to acknowledge that we need to connect with our people. We need their presence to stay on our path, and they need ours.

We yearn for soul buddies our whole lives and often we have to find ourselves before they can find us.

When you find the way
Others will find you
Passing by on the road
They will be drawn to your door
The way that cannot be heard
will be reflected in your voice
The way that cannot be seen
Will be reflected in your eyes

—Lao Tzu

STARS IN THE SKY

There is room in the heart for all the affections, as there is room in heaven for all the stars.

—Victor Hugo

Some relationships are forever, but some are just for a season, because we share the same location and space for that certain amount of time.

We all have many seasons in our lives: home, school, college, vacations, jobs, our children and the relationships we form through them, clubs and activities, sports, church, gym.

When those seasons change, some friendships endure, but many of them don't. And it's normal. I didn't always understand this. Often, losing a friendship felt like a failure on my part—I was not enough, I didn't try enough—when it was just a natural part of the cycle of life. Even when I was the one actively trying to distance myself from a relationship I had encouraged, I was overwhelmed with guilt. "Why did I engage in this relationship if it feels so wrong now?"

What I have come to understand is that those people came into our life for a reason at that specific time. Remember that spring flower that welcomed you one morning as you were leaving your house with a hurried and heavy heart? It was meant to bloom that very morning to light up your day. Even the friendships that ended on a bad note started out as a bright cheerful blossom on the doorsteps of that time in our lives.

> *I've learned that people will forget what you said, people will forget what you did, but people will never forget how you made them feel.*
>
> —Maya Angelou

I'll never forget how all those people made me feel:

My best college and post-college friend who shared all my dreams and struggles. We supported each other through painful uncertain times, but when we both started to blossom and find our way, we drifted away from each other. Strangely, some friendships will nurture and support us through our misery but not our joys.

All the work colleagues whose morning smiles, chats around the coffee-machine and advice were my lifeline in that confined environment, but faded away when I left that world.

All the mothers and fathers who were my steady companions for over twenty-five years of raising children. Most of the time, all we had in common were our children, but nothing else was needed. All those parents I only saw on the soccer, baseball, football fields, at wrestling matches, Girls and Cubs Scouts meetings, who were more a part of our lives than our own family at that time. People whose number I had on speed dial but whose names I would probably not remember now.

The friend with whom I shared a life-changing spiritual journey which guided us into opposite directions. Our passionate discussions helped me to discover my true path. We now agree to disagree. With great love.

The friends who just wear us out. We call them toxic, but sometimes they're just needy. We fall in love with their intensity but this ride with them never goes very far. They drain us. At the risk of losing ourselves in the repetitive play of their drama, a time comes when we have to let them go.

The friend who encouraged me to teach yoga. Sadly, we did not share the same values and we lost the friendship. How ironic that he was the one who inspired me to make one of the most important decisions of my life! The lights that guide us toward our most meaningful transformations often come from the most unlikely sources.

And the most dangerous kind: the spider friends. They lure us into their lives with sweet words of praise and control us with those pats on the back that make us feel so good. Unconsciously, we want to please them to keep that positive reinforcement going. But as soon as our agenda doesn't fit theirs any longer and we show signs of leaving their sweet trap, they sting us with sharp venomous words meant to hurt. We think that they are our biggest supporters, the ones we can always count on, but they can turn on us with unexpected rage. Bitterness coated in sugar.

It took me a while to learn this life lesson. A true friend does not try to control us, does not judge us and doesn't criticize us for following our dreams. This is a very valuable lesson learned from experience that keeps us from falling into the sweet trap of a controlling relationship.

The key is to keep company only with people who uplift you, whose presence calls forth your best.

—Epictetus

Some friends are only a phone call away, several states or a whole continent away, a warm welcome stop on a road or plane trip. They are home away from home.

Some live only a few miles away, but we're taking a break, our weekly lunches a distant memory. They're still here, just not as present.

Some are lost forever. No desire to see each other again. Ever. The season was short, but still had its purpose.

I like to think of all those friendships, even the ones we would rather forget, as stars in the sky. So many of them, some brighter than others, some mere twinkles in the distance, some shooting stars, but all of them with a relevance that shaped the landscape of our own personal universe.

FOUR POINTS

My lesson, after five decades, is to finally accept that not everything has to be forever.

Why not, whispers the idealistic me?

First of all, just like a love affair, the novelty and intensity of a profound all-consuming friendship cannot be sustained forever. And, without the fire, some friendships just die.

Second, there would be no room for new friends if we kept all our old ones on the same level. Just like there is no room in our closet for another pair of black yoga pants until we have let go of an old pair.

Third, we grow and change because there are seasons in life as in nature. As Bruce Barton said: *When you are through changing, you are through.* Our friends will not necessarily change and grow at the same time we do, and those moments are crossroads when we each go our separate ways.

Fourth and last, all of those friendships are a lesson, especially the ones that end badly, the ones we wish had never happened.

I can remember vividly when the important relationships in my life ended. I can still taste the pain and loss. Some ended gradually, some with a bang. Some ended to make room for a new life and new friends. Some ended and left a void I thought I would never fill. Some losses were welcome, some were a complete shock.

Now in my fifties, I realize that it all happened for a reason and that those gaps in the road were mapping out the life I have now.

LETTING IT FLOW

Be still like a mountain and flow like a great river.

—Lao Tzu

Recently, I have found myself reconnecting with several of my childhood friends, people who, I thought, were lost forever and had long forgotten me. Now they are letting me know I was always a part of their memories.

Three years ago, seeing and hugging my dearest childhood friends, Marielle and Thierry, was a clear, indescribable joy, as pure as our young friendship was over thirty years ago. They had found me on social media.

Our interrupted journey resumes…

* * *

Like water in our sacral chakra, friendships once again float toward us and we can welcome them again into our lives from where we are, opening ourselves to whom they have become.

Like water, relationships are fluid. They come and go, like the ebb and flow of the ocean.

Like water, we cannot control them. Just enjoy their tides, high and low.

Like water, they feed the seeds of our lives and help them grow.

Like water, they can be treacherous and we have to know how to come up for breath when we sink too deep.

Like water, we let them flow and trickle between our fingers.

Like water, we cannot live without them.

2. THE SACRAL CHAKRA: SVADHISHTHANA

COLOR: Orange
TRANSLATION: Sweetness
LOCATION: Four finger widths below navel

KEY WORDS:
Sensing, Emotions, Pleasure, Sexuality, Relationships, Nourishment

RELATED BODY PARTS:
Pelvis, Hips, Sacrum, Reproductive System, Kidney, Bladder, Prostate, Blood

QUALITIES WHEN BALANCED:
Ability to Sense and Feel, Ease with Intimacy and Sexuality, Fluidity, Ability to Handle Change, Creativity, Enthusiasm and Joy, Vibrancy, No Addiction

PSYCHOLOGICAL SIGNS OF IMBALANCE:
Intimacy Issues, Shyness, Jealousy, Obsessions, Compulsions and Addictions (eating), Numbness, Neediness, Isolation, Co-Dependence

PHYSICAL SIGNS OF IMBALANCE:
Problems with Reproductive/Sexual Organs; Uterine, Bladder, Prostate or Kidney Trouble, Low Back Pain

POSITIVE ARCHETYPE: The Ruler
NEGATIVE ARCHETYPE: The Martyr
ELEMENT: Water
SENSE: Taste
SOUND: VAM
VERB: I Feel
FOOD: Liquids

HEALING TOOLS

Self-study:

- What childhood or teenage relationships do you remember most vividly?

- Do you have "bookend relationships"?

- Did you have angels in your life? Have you been an angel to someone?

- Have you met/do you have soul buddies?

- Do you have a relationship that is your rock?

- Are any relationships in your current life draining you?

- Did you—or do you—have "spider friends"?

- Is it difficult for you to let go of relationships?

- Do you have a hard time with changes?

- Do you try to hide or control your feelings?

Practical tools:
- Reconnect with an old friend
- Set time aside for the friends in your life: a walk, a lunch date
- Tell your friends you appreciate them
- Wear orange, place orange flowers, a bowl of oranges or orange items in your home
- Do a walking meditation in the water
- Do a seated meditation near open water
- Watch the moon, meditate under moonlight
- Do something creative, explore your creativity
- Embrace new sensations: taste/cook new food
- Embrace your sensuality: take scented baths, use scented oils
- Dance: belly-dancing, tango, salsa
- Move freely, feel good in your body
- Go swimming or practice other water activities
- Get a full body massage or a lymphatic massage
- Study and practice Tantra Yoga
- Practice Tai Chi
- Practice Vinyasa (Flow) Yoga
- Practice Pranayama: Ida Nadi (Alternate Nostril Breath)

ASANAS: Cat and Cow, Hip Openers (Pigeon, Butterfly), Forward Bends, Cobra, Yin Yoga, Moon Salutations, Seated and Standing Pelvic Circles

MANTRA: *I Move and Live with Fluidity*

SACRAL CHAKRA MEDITATION

Find a comfortable place where you feel safe and grounded
Sitting or lying down
Relaxing into the body and into the breath
Sending the breath to that space between lower belly and sacrum
The breath is a beautiful orange light that nourishes and warms your
    sacrum
Repeating your Mantra: *I Move and Live with Fluidity*
Starting to visualize yourself walking through the woods
It feels good to move your body and become the rhythm of each step
I Move and Live with Fluidity
Soon you start hearing a soothing magical sound
The sound of rushing water
You follow that sound and what it promises
It's growing louder
And you come upon a majestic waterfall
Tumbling from rocks sprinkled with bright orange flowers
Your senses are awakened
You need to taste and feel the water
You take off your clothes, take off your inhibitions
And step into the pool of water under the waterfall
Absorbing its coolness in your feet and legs
As you walk closer to the cascading froth
I Move and Live with Fluidity
Now you are under the waterfall
Wrapped in its refreshing sensual liquid touch
Allowing the water to stroke and explore every part of your body
Opening your mouth to taste it on your tongue
Trickling down your shoulders, back, chest, belly and legs

Feeling it on your skin

Deep in your muscles and bones

Reaching every single cell of your being

I Move and Live with Fluidity

Allowing the water to cleanse your mind and heart from worries and
pain

I Move and Live with Fluidity

Feeling the vibrancy and joy of the water flowing through your most
intimate parts

All the corners of your soul

I Move and Live with Fluidity

As you abandon yourself to the flow of the water

Promising yourself to surrender to the flow of life

Promising yourself to feel, taste and surrender to beautiful vibrant
creative You

I Move and Live with Fluidity.

CHAPTER 3

MANIPURA
SOLAR PLEXUS CHAKRA

Do not surrender your power to others

We must be willing to let go of the life we had planned so as to have the life that is waiting for us.

—Joseph Campbell

Firmly anchored into the world of family and relationships, we are now able to grow deeper into Manipura, our personal power center. This is where we build our self-esteem and start our transformation from within. In this chakra, we build our inner fire; not only our physical fire—metabolism and stamina—but the flame of our will and autonomy. Confident in our own abilities, we have enough will power to act on them to start our true journey. It is a difficult rite of passage because we will face criticism as we leave old ways behind in order to find our own voice. The key is to start our inner fire. Once we overcome our doubts and inertia and start moving, Manipura kicks in and we come into our own power with ease and grace. The only way to true liberation is through our inner energy becoming action. The main obstacle on this path will be judgment.

JUDGMENT

If you judge people, you have no time to love them.

—Mother Teresa

Everyone's most inherent wish is to be loved and accepted.

But we profoundly misunderstand this concept. We think we have to be accepted—who we are and everything we do—in order to be loved, when in truth love is absolutely and unilaterally unconditional.

Love doesn't have any restrictions. People who truly love us accept us as we are.

Then why is one of society's favorite pastime this need to judge, criticize, desiccate and tear apart the details of others' lives? We do it to celebrities we don't even know and who have absolutely no relevance in our lives, and to people around us, some of whom we also hardly know.

Who are we to judge?

Who are we to tell people how they should live their lives?

Are our own lives so small, so devoid of meaning, that we have time to comment on and rearrange other people's existence?

I have witnessed and experienced the destructive and evil effects of judgmental and gossipy comments since I was a little girl, eavesdropping on adults' conversations.

Some were funny, but at whose expense?

Some were spiteful about people I really liked. Why?

Most were random and meaningless. Who cared what that person wore, who they were sleeping with, or how much money they had or did not have?

I didn't understand. Why waste time talking about what others were doing? Let them figure it out by themselves. Or tell them in a more constructive way.

I was much more interested planning my own life and finding the roads that would lead me to it. I didn't have time to worry about other people.

I was also deeply unsettled by the random cruelty of those words that could destroy someone's hopes and character. This need to criticize and mock others seemed to come from a profound weakness and doubt in one's own power.

I promised myself back then that I would never let what anyone said about me—however much it hurt—affect who I was and what I wanted to be and do.

I've been told that I was an easy child, so trustworthy that I could be left alone at a very young age, sitting on the open windowsill in my grandparents' second floor kitchen without any worry. I played by myself for hours. I didn't have tantrums, probably because I thought, even back then, that they were a waste of precious energy.

The first of many grandchildren, I probably soaked up lots of love in those early years, like flowers that instinctively soak in light and then, when the sun does not shine any longer, still blossom and grow. I was not spoiled and did not demand attention. I was content.

Well aware that my world was small and contained and that I had plenty to learn, I listened. Listened and made up my mind back then that adults talked a lot of nonsense and that I would only keep what fit my purpose.

By listening, I also learned that people love to tear apart others' dreams, and I was not going to let anyone do that to me. If what I said and did was going to be judged, it was safer to keep it to myself.

What I believed only belonged to me.

The quiet battle to keep my own power began.

COURAGE AGAINST THE MIRROR OF OTHERS

We are spending so much time and energy being afraid that we're not fully walking into our powers and gifts.

—Brene Brown

My mother is the most courageous person I know.

In her environment, she is Super Woman.

As the oldest and only girl in a family of six, she helped care for her five brothers through the Second World War and postwar France. She graduated from high school—not a small accomplishment for a village girl in France in the fifties—but had to go to work immediately to help her family. Her father did not treat her well; neither did her husband nor some of her brothers. Her first baby died shortly after birth and her third child, my brother Patrice, died of cancer at twenty-six. She lost her two boys. I am her only remaining child.

She worked full-time as an army civilian employee, raised two children, maintained a garden, made jams and canned food, cooked and baked everything from scratch, knitted and needle-pointed like a professional, was church organist and choir director, prepared baptisms and funerals, and was president and volunteer in countless organizations—her union, the Red Cross, village library, women's gymnastics, to name a few. She was a journalist/photographer for three regional papers, an elected official for most of her life: council member and deputy mayor, as well as the official historian of her village, with archives most libraries would envy.

When I prepared posters to commemorate her life for her eightieth birthday in 2015, I had to use several boards to list only a small part of all her achievements.

Even though she can hardly walk due to knee issues, up until last year she still maintained a garden that could feed ten families.

She is also more selfless and generous than I can ever aspire to be. She visited the sick in her parish, delivered get-well baskets, nursed my brother, my great-aunt, my great-uncle, my father and countless others when they were sick and dying.

I could not do a quarter of what she has done in her life.

Yet, this amazing woman has spent her entire life worrying about "what people think."

I understand that this might be a small-town thing, a generational thing, or even a French thing.

What I never understood was why my mother—this super woman—let others rob her of her own power. I would see her thrive when she was praised and appreciated, and crumble when people—out of pure spite and jealousy—tried to bring her down.

They would criticize her weight; the surest and most cowardly way to demean a woman. She is beautiful, but has always been openly self-conscious about her size, even when she was just "pleasantly plump." Some of her brothers, as well as her opponents in the political world or the village, used it against her. My father would call her "fat names" when he was mad at her.

What did her weight have to do with anything? She was stronger and had more endurance than most men.

I was so struck by the futility of this obsession that, to this day, I never question my weight or anyone's weight. I don't talk about it. I don't comment on people losing weight or gaining weight. It is one's business, one's private affair, one's own body. What really matters is how strong and healthy one feels. My youngest cousin Josselin, who was staying with us several years ago when he was thirteen, told me that I was the only woman he knew who didn't talk about "dieting" or "needing to go on a diet." He called it "refreshing." I call it a lesson learned from watching Maman suffer from those attacks.

Several years ago, a book called *French women don't get fat* came out. I had to smile. Because, in "my France," French women felt fat, talked about it obsessively and were always either dieting or talking about dieting. Even when they did not need to.

Sadly, Maman was part of that society obsessed with thinness and started to accept the "fat" label, however much it hurt.

She would say: "I don't care."

But she cared.

She still did what she had to do. But instead of owning the joy she deserved, she let others' opinions and judgments define her joy.

Whatever she accomplished, she needed the mirror of those others to reflect her own worth, when it was there the whole time.

When they approved of her, she was elated.

When they didn't, she was crushed.

She allowed others to create limitations for her life.

Fight for your limitations and you get to keep them.

—Baron Baptiste

She tried to use that mirror on me, with her words more than her actions, wanting me to conform to the norm around her, not realizing that she was trying to stop me from being myself.

I was a tomboy and all I wanted to wear were shorts and tank tops, but she wanted me to dress a certain way—like a proper young lady, older than my age—refusing to take me with her if I didn't look right.

She wanted me to have the right friends.

She wanted me to spend less time in my books and more time socializing.

She wanted me to do what "others" approved of at the time, in her world.

She wanted me to find a proper job close to home instead of wasting my time on what she thought were useless travels.

She questioned my decisions, and her criticism made me question myself.

But not for long.

I didn't have much regard for what people thought.

I didn't care if it was a French thing, or a village thing, or a generational thing.

But it was definitely not my thing.

I only had one life and I was not going to let anyone tell me how to live it.

I understood that my mother, who had trailblazed her own way, was afraid for me.

Afraid that, like her, I would be criticized and judged.

She did not understand why I had no desire to fit in her world.

In her world, she was Super Woman.

I had to go and be Super Woman in my own world.

Even if I had to fight for it.

Then I would come back.

And I would help her escape all her limitations.

And I did. Over the years, I have taken her to places she used to dream about, places she thought she would never see: Bavaria, King Ludwig's castles, Austria, the United States, Panama, and the latest, to celebrate her eightieth birthday, a Caribbean cruise.

But what touches me the most is to see my daughter continue the tradition, taking her grandmother on grand adventures; to Provence, to a classy hotel on the Nice seafront or to the pubs of Ireland.

Because she knows, just like me, that someone who has accomplished so much against so many odds deserves to live the full dimension of her life.

THE QUIET BATTLE

Dare to be yourself.

—André Gide

Up until my teenage years, I had been used to praises: the good, studious little girl. I loved my small, private middle school, Sainte-Marie, where everyone seemed focused on learning. But with boarding high school in Sacré-Coeur, I entered a brutal, merciless arena that shocked and startled me. I came from a small world, where I had successfully protected myself, and I was not ready for this larger, crueler world.

All of a sudden, I found out I did not wear the right clothes, I was not cool enough and did not have the right friends. It was a huge blow to my self-esteem that had not really been scarred yet and, for a while, I tried to fit in, wear the hippy clothes that were popular in the late seventies, even smoke for a few seconds (two cigarettes and I was done), hang out with people I did not relate to. One cannot win in this game! I was miserable and I almost lost myself.

Then, for probably the first time in my life, I rebelled openly and gave up the pretense. Why should I care about this crowd? They would always find something wrong with me anyway. I knew this period would be over soon and would definitely not be the highlight of my life. I made one important resolution that influenced the rest of my life: I accepted being an outsider and I focused on my studies and a very small group of friends who seemed to share my values. This was accompanied with another decision that brought me criticism: I decided to not pursue the scientific field, but to instead enroll in the literary/linguistic branch, which is less valued in the French academic system. I wanted to do what I really loved.

Once I made those decisions, I felt liberated and fairly happy in what had been a miserable period in my life.

Buddhism teaches us that no one else controls our destiny. It's all in our hands. I did not know about Buddhism back then, but I was choosing to live by those principles.

One of my fondest memories was at the end of our second high school year (French high school only lasts three years, middle school four.) A group of us asked permission to stay behind to study for the first part of our Baccalauréat (French high school diploma). Our small group: five of us—three girls, two boys—had the whole school to ourselves. We would eat together in the empty cafeteria and study all day long in empty classrooms, discussing literature and philosophy. This earned us the reputation of the biggest nerds in the school for wanting to stay in during the break, but to me, this was heaven!

* * *

Unlike most French families, we did not go on summer vacations. My parents thought traveling was frivolous.

Strangely, those long summer months—riding my bicycle through our village's sun-drenched deserted streets, waiting for my friends to return, tanned and full of stories about their exciting vacations—did not make me bitter. Instead they empowered me. Gave me the hunger to discover the world on my own, not because someone was bringing me along, but because I would create the opportunity myself.

My parents gave me the biggest gift of not taking anything for granted.

During those lonely summer months, I read, studied, wrote and prepared myself for the life I was meant to live.

Picking a university was easy: I loved languages and I wanted to travel, so I enrolled in the Lyon Catholic University Translators' school where students were required to spend their first year in England and their last year in Germany. My parents did not mind my trips to England because this was part of my education, but they did not approve when I started traveling on my own during the summer. I understood their concerns, but I had to create my own experiences. Air travel was still expensive back then in the early eighties, so most European youth could only afford to travel by train with special discounted passes. I tutored during the year and worked part of the summer to pay for my trips. I wanted my younger brother to have that experience as well and I took him with me on one of my trips to England. We had to do it on the cheap, riding trains, buses and ferries from Lyon to Paris to London, but it opened his eyes to the world. After he became a chef, he worked and lived abroad; his first job was in London.

At twenty, when I told my parents I was traveling three days and two nights by train to Norway to visit the family of my pen pal, they threatened and complained, but I did not budge. My mother told me that I was *inconsciente*—her favorite word to describe my lack of sense at the time—and proceeded to tell me in lurid details how I would be robbed, raped and killed.

My grandfather, who always supported my adventures—he had taken me to Marseille on several May 1st celebrations (Fête du Travail: our French Labor Day) and on my first trip to Paris when I was fifteen—accompanied me to the capital, where I took the night train to Copenhagen. This was the first leg of my journey to Mosjøen, which I would reach three days later, after crossing Germany, Denmark, Sweden and half of Norway.

I will never forget this journey, the people I met, the incredible scenery, the joy of finally arriving and spending a month with this family who opened their hearts and home to me, and became an important part of my life. I learned Norwegian and returned the following year. This solo trip made me the traveler I am today—connecting to the people, sounds and rhythms of a culture, instead of hurried tours of cities and sites to check items off a bucket list. It also taught me that facing one's fears is the only way to grow.

THE RISK TO BLOSSOM

The day comes when the risk to remain tight in a bud is more painful than the risk it takes to blossom.

—Anais Nin

After my last year of study in Germany, I spent three months in Cambridge, England to work on my final dissertation on the poet Rupert Brooke. I had asked and been invited to the King's College Library to use the poet's unpublished letters and material, a glorious memory, tinged with regrets. I don't have many regrets but one of the few in my life is to have listened to that odious little voice: "Who do you think you are?" when it was suggested that I publish this thesis. I did not do it. Creating my own limitations.

Or perhaps, my battle lay elsewhere that year.

The next few months undoubtedly determined the rest of my life.

A month after my return to France, Mémé passed unexpectedly of a stroke at sixty-nine. My family was in disarray. It was my first loss. I had never known such pain.

I remember applying rouge on her cold cheeks and lipstick on her dry lips before the funeral, because I knew she would have wanted to look her best. Just like when she had company.

After the funeral, the family doctor announced in front of the whole family that my grandfather was too distraught to stay by himself and needed full time attention.

I remember this moment so vividly, as we all stood under the big plane tree in my grandparents' pebbled front yard on this unusually warm February afternoon.

My relatives gathering around the doctor, sad and solicitous.

Maman's grief-stricken face, as she stood back. She had lost her best friend.

Pépé, slumped over his chair, tears glistening on his old cheeks.

Everything in slow motion, as if the universe was setting up the stage for the rest of my life.

"He needs someone to take care of him for a couple of months. And he wants just one person."

My relatives nodding approval.

"He wants his granddaughter, his *Titi*."

I had been looking up at the sky. Sun piercing through the clouds. Leaves rustling in the wind.

Now looking down; everyone staring at me.

My relatives with shock and disbelief.

Maman with pained anger. She had never understood my closeness with Pépé, who had always treated her so callously.

Papa with amusement. He had always been the outsider, and now his daughter was the "chosen one."

"Are you able to do that, Mademoiselle?"

Noises. My relatives voicing their concern.

"She can't, she's at university. Aren't you, Christine?"

Stepping forward: "I'm available. I've finished school. I'll be writing my dissertation the next few months, and I can easily do it here."

My grandfather, smiling up at me.

He wanted to get away. So, we traveled the railroads of France for several weeks.

Lourdes to visit *La Sainte Vierge* and to pray for my grandmother. Everyone knew him there, because of his volunteer work; he was a celebrity.

Paris, because he loved Paris. His birthplace.

I learned a lot during this journey. It was a rite of passage. I mourned my Mémé and her gentle spirit, and knew she would always be the angel on my shoulder. But I also learned that my Pépé was imperfect. The rumors were true; he was cheating. I met his kind, soft-spoken lady friend in Paris. But it was not for me to judge; he had loved my grandmother in his own way. He owned his imperfections and didn't try to validate his life with excuses. No one ever had nor ever could take his power away from him.

When we came back to our village, my relatives' disapproval was palpable. They believed my grandfather should have grieved in his own home instead of traveling around the country with me.

For the next few weeks I spent most of my time at his house. I helped him get used to his new life without Mémé and I finished my thesis. My mentor gave me high praises, but nobody cared. I had to get serious and find a real life, a real job.

Out of duty, I tried for a few months to fit the mold my parents had for me. I even rented an apartment in Lyon with a friend and looked for a job there while freelancing as a typist and tutor.

I knew I was at a crossroad. I could either stay on the safer straight path or I could take that turn that led into the unknown.

All I knew was that I felt completely disconnected from whom I wanted to be.

I could not breathe.

I needed to go back to the world meant for me. Out there.

Before life became a series of limitations.

I took the turn and did the unthinkable. I took a trip to America.

Once again, my grandfather saved me; he rode the train with me all the way to Brussels where I took my first flight to the United States. I spent one and a half months there with friends and in Quebec with my uncle and his family—who lived there at the time—riding Greyhound buses from Texas to Montreal, and back to Texas, carrying my suitcases…

My parents had stopped talking to me, until they received a phone call from my future employer. Before I left, I had sent my resume to this particular French corporate bank, and their Hamburg branch was requesting my services. Maman phoned me in Montreal, where I was staying. I took an early flight back to France, packed my bags and moved to Hamburg to start my new life. With four suitcases.

Once again, my grandfather was the one who rode the train with me as far as Geneva, where he helped me get settled on the train to Zurich. I would make my connection to Hamburg there. Alone. With my four suitcases.

Traveling was not easy.

But it was my choice.

I had been carrying those suitcases all by myself since I had made the decision to own my life.

Every time I arrived in a new place, there was always uncertainty.

The battle to own our power is not an easy one.

It often goes against the grain.

It often makes us feel that we are a foot soldier while everyone around us rides a horse. But the foot soldier can maneuver her way around the horses, trampling through the mud, getting dirty, yet making her way to the heart of the battle.

Throughout my years of studies in England and Germany, I had been a penniless student and I lived like one. I remember someone asking me once why I always wore the same clothes; they were all I had and I would rather spend money on books and theater tickets than on clothing. When I started working in Hamburg in the mid-eighties, I lived in a tiny studio, with neither phone nor television. When I moved to Frankfurt six months later, I slept on my friend's floor for two months until I found my own studio behind the Hauptbahnhof.

During that time, I heard that my father never talked about me because he did not know what to say. I lived abroad in a country he did not approve of, among strangers he did not know, speaking languages he did not understand, doing adult things he did not want to think about.

My mother would tell me stories of girls my age who were not only married, but had their own house, car, dishwasher and children. Her way to persuade me that my traveling was a waste of time and money, because I had none of those.

I acquired those later—and more—but they do not define who I am.

Who I am was shaped during those moments of quiet courage when I dragged my four suitcases across dark, dirty train platforms throughout Europe, when I embarked on traveling ventures in a world that had neither cell phones nor Internet, when I spent long nights in dingy bus stations, airport lounges or on deserted train platforms, too scared to sleep.

I am so glad I fought for those scary moments, instead of fighting for limitations.

* * *

Last year, after we took Maman on our family cruise, she spent a month with us in Virginia. We had a lovely time; she reminisced about the past a lot, especially about Papa. One afternoon while I was preparing dinner, she sat in her usual spot on our corner bench, knitting a scarf for Patou, my youngest. She looked up at me with a smile and said: "You know, your father and I, when we got married, we could never have imagined that we would one day have a daughter like you."

My quiet battle had ended.

As we let our light shine, we unconsciously give other people permission to do the same. As we are liberated from our own fears, our own presence actually liberates others.

—Marianne Williamson

THE FOUR SUITCASES

Looking back, I know I did not always carry those suitcases very gracefully.

My shoulders were hunched under the weight.

My face was red, my hair disheveled and my breath ragged from the exertion.

I took some wrong turns, but I never gave up.

I knew I was on the right path because, along the corridors of my journey, I started to carry them with more ease, poise and skill.

My first suitcase used to be extremely heavy because it carried my arrogance. I used it as an armor to protect myself until I realized that healthy self-respect is not prideful; it is humble. My case is lighter now that it is filled with caring confidence.

My second suitcase was tough to open; it carried my stubbornness. Stubbornness can create limitations of its own, but discipline—its gentler cousin—creates possibilities. Discipline helps me to unlock what seems impossible.

My third suitcase had several handles. Anyone could grab a handle from any side. I was often wary of anyone offering help, sometimes with good reasons. But, with time, I learned to trust, to accept, and even to ask for help. Those handles represented all the opportunities offered to me so many times. Those opportunities became experiences.

I was ashamed of my fourth suitcase; it was old and battered, of a strange amber color that showed stains. This was the piece of luggage I would have liked to leave behind because its appearance was embarrassing. But strangely, it was the one that contained everything I really needed. It was filled with memories, happy and sad, as well as joyful, silly moments. It was a reminder to honor our differences and not to take ourselves too seriously, especially when we are on the journey of our life.

Our battered suitcases were piled on the sidewalk again;
we had longer ways to go.
But no matter, the road is life.

—Jack Kerouac

3. THE SOLAR PLEXUS CHAKRA: MANIPURA

COLOR: Yellow
TRANSLATION: City of Gems
LOCATION: Navel to Solar Plexus
KEY WORDS: Will Power, Self-Esteem

RELATED BODY PARTS:
Pancreas, Liver, Digestive System, Stomach, Gall Bladder, Spleen

QUALITIES WHEN BALANCED:
Vitality, Strength of Will, Sense of Purpose and Self-Worth, Growth, Effectiveness, Authenticity, Cooperation, Commitment, Non-judgment, Personal Honor, Responsibility to Make Decisions, Humor

PSYCHOLOGICAL SIGNS OF IMBALANCE:
Lack of Direction, Inability to Slow down, Low Self-Esteem or Narcissism, Attachment to Status and Fame, Lack of Values, Competition, Prejudice, Judgment, Intimidation, Submission, Rage, Shame, Depression, Disempowerment, "Butterflies" in Stomach, Stress, Self-Loathing, Indifference, Wastefulness

PHYSICAL SIGNS OF IMBALANCE:
Digestive problems, Inflammation, Ulcers, Pancreas and Liver Problems, Hypertension, Obesity, Hypoglycemia, Diabetes

POSITIVE ARCHETYPE: The Warrior
NEGATIVE ARCHETYPE: The Servant
ELEMENT: Fire
SENSE: Sight
SOUND: RAM
VERB: I Can
FOOD: Starches, Grains

HEALING TOOLS

Self-study:

- Do you let others' judgments affect you?

- Do you judge others? Why?

- Do you own your power?

- Do you fight for your power or your limitations?

- What are your greatest strengths?

- When do you feel most aligned with your own power?

- Give an example of a situation when you felt fully empowered.

- Are you living the life you were meant to have?

- What are your four suitcases?

Practical tools:

- Think of a project that is important to you, that represents your intrinsic values and that you always wanted to start and/or complete. Begin planning an outline for this project
- Engage in an activity that makes you laugh (read, watch comedy, play with pets or children) and have a big belly laugh
- Take classes or read books that empower you
- Do mind puzzles
- Bring the color yellow into your life: clothing, a scarf, a bowl of lemons, yellow flowers, sunflowers
- Practice discipline: meditate at the same time every day
- Spend time in the sun
- Connect to the fire element: sit by a fireplace, have candles around your house
- Try belly-dancing
- Vigorous yoga practices to develop personal power
- Think of engaging your core throughout the day: press navel to spine and hold
- Core work
- Power Walk
- Practice Yoga Nidra relaxation to reduce stress
- Conscious breathing: breathe from the belly
- Kapalabhati (Breath of Fire)

ASANAS: Spinal Twists (especially Standing Twists), Bridge, Backbends, Plank, Chair, Warriors, Sun Salutations, Stomach Crunches, Core Work, Boat

MANTRA: *I Own and Honor my Power*

SOLAR PLEXUS MEDITATION

Find a comfortable place where you feel safe and grounded
Sitting or lying down
Relaxing into the body and into the breath
Sending the breath to the belly
The breath is a beautiful yellow light that nourishes and warms your
  belly
Repeating your Mantra: *I Own and Honor my Power*
Starting to visualize yourself climbing a mountain
The climb is steep. The terrain is rough
You're carrying a heavy backpack
Feeling its weight on your shoulders, the way they're hunched under its
  weight
Your whole body aches and your breath is ragged, but you keep walking
Slow and steady up the steep mountain
All you can see is the ground, the dirt, the rocks
Your feet slip on those rocks, but naturally return to balance and the
  patient climb
One step at a time
One insidious thought is creeping into your mind: What's the point?
  What's the purpose of this climb?
You observe the thought, without judgment
You allow it to slowly flow
Flowing through your mind and out of your mind
You know your purpose
I Own and Honor my Power
You begin to surrender to the rhythm of the climb, each step more
  assured, each breath more steadfast
I Own and Honor my Power
Suddenly the ground feels more even, and your back slowly straightens,
  one vertebra at a time, until you're standing perfectly upright
At the top of the mountain

You are not looking down any longer, you're looking up
Up toward the sky and the glorious sun shining brightly on you
I Own and Honor my Power
There is no difference between you and the sun
Its magnificence is your magnificence
You feel the weight on your shoulders
And realize you don't need your backpack any longer
Very slowly, you remove one strap from one shoulder, and the other
strap from the other shoulder
You let the heavy backpack fall to the ground
You feel free
As you let go of burdens, judgment and doubts
As you acknowledge your power and your purpose
Standing at the top of the mountain
Looking up at the sky, and at the beauty of the world all around you
Bathing in the glory of the sun
And the certainty of who you are
I Own and Honor my Power.

CHAPTER 4

ANAHATA
HEART CHAKRA

Just forgive

Forgiveness isn't about the other person.
It's about us.
It's about allowing ourselves to heal, to move on and to let the experience change
us in a positive way.
There will always be love and light if you open that door.
When we allow ourselves to finally forgive, let go and make peace with a situation
that cannot be changed, we give ourselves the freedom to love others and love life
again.

—B. Uyemura

Anahata is at the center of our being, physically and emotionally.

It is the bridge between the lower chakras, the strong roots that help us create our place in this world, and the upper chakras, which help us to define and project our deeper truths. Nothing feels more healing than resting in our heart center, universal symbol of love and emotional power. This is the time to be genuine and lay bare our most embarrassing wounds. This is the place where we finely tune our emotions to our own inner music.

When our heart chakra is out of balance, we're disconnected from our humanity and from our true purpose. We feel separated, both from ourselves and from the world.

The Buddha said that separation is the cause of suffering.

When our heart breaks, we feel alone and powerless. We suffer. Nothing seems to help. It's easy to lose ourselves, lose sight of who we truly are, lose sight of our essence.

* * *

As I am writing this, my home country was just struck by tragedy when a band of cowardly fanatics attacked and slaughtered dozens of innocent victims in Paris, people who were doing what French people do on a Friday evening: eating out, attending a concert or a soccer game.

They attacked normalcy.

They attacked all of us at the core of our beings as they tried to rob us of our peace of mind.

In the face of such random horror, as a coping mechanism, pain quickly and understandably transforms itself into anger. And anger can very easily become pure hatred. Hating seems the only way to fight back.

Several of my friends back home told me that they had never felt such rage and it scared them. Their peaceful selves did not know how to handle such random violence and they wanted to strike back. Forgiveness was not even on their radar. One friend told me: "One can only pull on the bow string so far…"

But isn't our rage exactly what those monsters want?

They want to destroy our humanity and bring us down to their levels.

A LESSON FROM DUMAS

Edmond Dantès: "I don't believe in God."
Abbé Faria: "It doesn't matter. He believes in you."
—Alexandre Dumas, *The Count of Monte-Cristo*

Originally, I called this chapter "Heartbreaks make us stronger," but now I feel I need to find a deeper lesson in this tragedy and in so many others.

Pain does make us stronger, but how will we use this strength—to hate or to love?

For most of my life, I fought pain with anger, hate and a visceral need for revenge. I thought it was the only way to remain strong and dignified, and survive. My favorite story was Alexandre Dumas' classic tale of vengeance: *The Count of Monte-Cristo*. My favorite part was Edmond Dantès' return to Parisian high society after his escape from Château d'If as the mysterious powerful Count, set upon taking his revenge on all those who grieved and betrayed him. I took immense pleasure in his well-crafted plots of retribution and their triumphant executions. It justified my own wishes for revenge. It gave me hope that injustices could and would be fixed.

I lost sight of the story's important final message. The Count's obsession for vengeance started to take over his life and he realized that it was not bringing him any peace. Fortunately, he stopped before it was too late. The story's ultimate lesson is mercy and forgiveness.

The joy that comes from revenge is not a healthy joy; it is just as twisted as the cruel actions that caused our pain.

It took me a long time to understand this.

* * *

A common misconception about forgiveness, which was mine, is to compare it to acceptance and resigned submission. Letting evil win.

After all, *The Count of Monte Cristo* would have been a pretty boring and unsatisfying story if Edmond had just forgiven those who had ruined him and stayed in his prison until he died. He had the right to repair injustice and fight for his freedom.

The lesson learned was that he should have done this without the hatred and bitterness that almost destroyed him and his innate goodness.

Forgiveness does not excuse evil behavior.

Forgiveness prevents this behavior from destroying our hearts.

* * *

One of my all-time heroes is Nelson Mandela. I remember my outrage when Mimi, my Senegalese college friend, told me of his long imprisonment. I didn't understand why the French news did not make his story a priority. I followed the long road to his release, and his election to the South African Presidency. I admired his grace as he began his fight for freedom, not as reprisal for the injustice that was done to him, but out of love for his countrymen.

He forgave so that he could move on and create positive changes: *As I walked out the door toward the gate that would lead to my freedom, I knew if I didn't leave my bitterness and hatred behind, I'd still be in prison.*

His life is a true example of triumphant forgiveness.

TRAGEDY

Your pain is the breaking of the shell that encloses your understanding.

—Kahlil Gibran

It took me a while to learn this lesson in my own life.

The most excruciating heartbreak of my life was the death of my twenty-six-year-old younger brother Patrice. As my only sibling, when I lost him, I lost a part of myself.

I felt alone.

I felt guilty for being the surviving child.

I felt powerless as I witnessed my parents' unbearable sorrow.

I also felt a sickening, overwhelming hatred for those who had abandoned and hurt him.

When Patrice had been diagnosed with liver cancer exactly two years before, our family had seemed concerned and supportive. I always thought they were the most reliable part of our lives. Of course, there were arguments, feuds, clashes of personalities, all rooted in Gaelic pride, but these people were blood and I believed they would always stand by us. After my grandmother had died unexpectedly five years previously, the foundation of our clan had crumbled ever so slightly. She had been the warm, selfless presence that held us together. Her unconditional love held us all accountable. Her death had left a huge void, but we'd made it through.

This time, we did not.

They—several of our relatives and friends—abandoned my brother and my parents ever so subtly, slowly, with valid excuses.

They did not like hospitals.

They were too busy.

They did what they could. And what could they do anyway?

Call us if you need anything…

* * *

I lived in New Jersey when Patrice was diagnosed in September 1990.

We had just spent one month all together in France at my parents' house. Patrice was taking his annual summer break from his demanding restaurant job in Brussels. At only twenty-four, he was already acquiring a reputation as a talented *saucier*, specializing in seafood sauces. He had big plans of continuing his career in the USA or Australia in the next few years; he was following his dream.

That summer was full of love, laughter and amazing food, days and nights blending into long evenings chatting on the terrace, with friends and relatives stopping by to join the fun, well into the early morning hours. Papa and Maman would also join us, relaxed and happy.

France-Lee, our little girl, adored her uncle, and he adored her. The two of them would disappear into the attic and return wearing colorful wigs and costumes, stuffing pillows under their shirts, improvising skits and imitations of some of the village's characters. I felt so grateful for my brother, the only person who understood my childhood, because he had lived it with me. I was looking forward to our continued dreams meshing together as our families would. I was looking forward to nieces and nephews, cousins for my children and many more summers just like this one. That summer was probably the happiest we ever had together.

* * *

Patrice never returned to his job, he never saw Brussels again.

* * *

I crossed the ocean often that first year after Patrice's diagnosis, with France-Lee, and then with my husband that first Christmas. Those trips were not easy, emotionally and financially, but I would have done anything to alleviate his suffering, to show him how much we loved and supported him.

Patrice underwent the most intense treatments—chemotherapy and radiation—which finally reduced the tumors enough to attempt surgery. To celebrate the success of the surgery, Patrice and Maman visited us in the States in September 1991, exactly one year after his diagnosis. This was a glorious visit, a celebration of hope and a new beginning. We toured the region: Cape May, New York, Philadelphia, the Amish Country, Gettysburg, Atlantic City, Washington DC, Maryland. I was also pregnant with our second child and Patrice was thrilled. He was certain it would be a boy, his first nephew. This was truly a new start for him and for our family.

Maman told me later that she knew it was just a short respite; the doctors had told them that two years was the most he could hope for. I did not know or, perhaps, I had chosen not to hear. My brother and I were making projects, building castles. He was a talented chef and, once he gained back his strength, he would move to the States and open a French restaurant. We would name it after my grandmother: *Chez Francine*. He wore his huge scar on his belly like a badge of honor. This scar would always remind him not to take life for granted. From now on, he would live the full expanse of his life. He would have no regrets.

When John, France-Lee and I moved to Panama a few months later, I felt confident that the worst was behind us. Patrice had given his blessing when we were considering this move, worried about even more geographical distance. He was excited for this new chapter in our lives.

Our little boy JC was born on February 6th, 1992, five days before Patrice's twenty-sixth birthday.

Before the Internet and Skype, expensive overseas phone calls were the only means of instant communication. When I called home to announce the birth, Patrice was excited, but I could hear the strain in his voice. He did not tell me, but Maman did. The cancerous tumors had come back.

I told him to hold on tight. I would be there in a few months, once everything was settled with the new baby.

Throughout all of this, most of my family at large had slowly withdrawn.

Few visits.

Few phone calls.

Little acknowledgment of the silent drama played out within the walls of my family home. My father could not cope: neither physically nor emotionally. After Patrice's diagnosis, he suffered a mini-stroke that left his left arm and leg semi paralyzed. He slowly became the shadow of the strong proud man he once was. He had already surrendered to the grasp of anger and despair, lashing out at the world and, unfortunately to all of us close to him.

He told me later that he had started dying when he heard his son had cancer.

To my family, our suffering was uncomfortable, almost indecent.

We were contagious.

This desertion hurt Patrice deeply. It became all he could think about, all he could talk about when he called me. I tried to reason with him, to focus on the positive, on us, on our strength.

But I could only stay neutral for so long.

Soon, his pain and anger started creeping into my psyche.

Soon, they became my own.

I could have handled being the one who was abandoned.

I could have handled my own pain.

But my brother's pain was unbearable.

I wanted to take it and make it mine and mine only.

What frightened me the most was that his anger would kill him. Not surprisingly, the liver is the seat of anger and I was afraid that his resentment would make things worse.

Resentment is like drinking poison and then hoping it will kill your enemies.

—Nelson Mandela

I told him to focus on healing and on all the people who loved him and were there for him.

He said all he could think about was the hurt of being abandoned by those people who were supposed to be "blood."

I told him to let it go. Write it down, all the injustice, all the wrong that was done to him. Write it all down. Release it all on paper. Cleanse himself.

He wrote it down, read it to me over the phone.

We cried together. Now he was free.

No, he told me. He was not free. It was not enough. He wanted the persons who had hurt him to know how much they had hurt him. He needed to send these letters.

Send them if it makes you free, I told him.

He sent them.

He said he felt free.

I thought that reading my brother's pain would make them see the error of their ways and they would apologize.

But instead, after those letters were sent, the relatives who had abandoned him felt they had a valid reason to do so, and the others started to feel vilified.

Knowing what I know now, I would ask him not to send those letters.

I know now that hate only begets hate.

I know now that we can only break the cycle of hate with love.

Darkness cannot drive out darkness: only light can do that.
Hate cannot drive out hate: only love can do that.

—Martin Luther King

But I was hurting too much to be wise.

Hurting too much to see clearly.

When I came back to France with France-Lee and my new baby that summer of 1992, Patrice was ecstatic to see us. For two months, we hung on to thin air, thin hope. We didn't believe the doctors when they told us there was not much more they could do. We could try radiation, but there was no guarantee.

Patrice did not want any more treatments.

He said he felt better.

He always felt better when we were home.

He would just heal himself.

Patrice got worse a few weeks after we left. My mother said he was in agony, hiding in the attic to scream in pain. The ambulance came. Hospital. Coma. Phone calls. The American Red Cross providing the four of us with plane tickets. Long flight from Panama. Layover in Brussels, Patrice's old hunting ground. A daze.

Patrice had woken up from his coma.

Just for us.

Everything was going to be all right. The miracle had happened. He was healed.

We visited him in Intensive Care. He was very yellow, but in great spirits. We talked, we laughed. He could not believe we had all come such a long way just to see him. I told him he had given us a big scare, but now that it was all over, we needed to make plans. The first thing he wanted to do was jump in water. Clear, clean, cool water. Dip his whole body into it, over and over again. A baptism of sort. Purifying himself of the sickness that had held him in her tight grip for the past two years.

We said goodbye. We would be back the next morning.

Phone call in the night.

Silent drive on the empty *autoroute*, John at the wheel.

The whole world asleep around us while our world shattered into a billion throbbing pieces of excruciating grief.

Papa in the passenger seat, his head hanging in raw pain.

Me and Maman in the backseat, feeling so powerless, holding her hand, so limp, so cold.

Everything so cold, the frantic walk through the empty hospital, the silence of the corridors, the solicitousness of the attendant, the room.

My brother on the bed.

So cold.

Stolen from us.

Gone.

To a warmer place, with waterfalls, streams and rivers…

* * *

I can say that I have known true heartbreak.

In this moment.

When I saw my brother, dead on a cold hospital bed at twenty-six.

When I saw my parents' indescribable unbearable pain, as they stood by their dead son's bed.

All I wanted to do was scream, scream, scream and never stop, hoping the screams would stop me from feeling.

FROM PAIN TO FORGIVENESS IN 4 STEPS

Forgiveness is the attribute of the strong.

—Mahatma Gandhi

I wish I had had the strength to forgive right away.

But anger is like a blanket that covers up our pain.

The pain was too intense.

So, I wrapped myself in that blanket.

Forgiving would have been easier if it had been just about my own grief. What I could not forgive was my brother's and my parents' suffering. I tried to cover it all up with the same blanket. But it was not big enough.

I was so uneducated in the rulebook of pain, and I took all the wrong turns: filling my heart with hatred, anger and righteousness.

Until I realized that this rage was just kindling for my pain.

It took me almost twenty years to learn to forgive completely, with four tiny baby steps that taught me one of the greatest lessons of my life.

1. *Easy Love*

First, we surrender to love.

Not love for the people we cannot yet forgive. But love for the good in our life. Love for the family that is still here. Love for the people who have never left our side.

They say that loving those who love us is the easy part, but when our heart is atrophied by pain, ease is what it needs. And that easy love is the first step toward healing.

* * *

Love for my husband who was rocking me to sleep when the tears would not stop.

Love for France-Lee, who was our bubble of light, our *rayon de soleil*. She was the only one who could make my parents smile.

Love for little JC, who needed me. Those quiet moments nursing him were my only moments of peace.

Love for my parents. I would have done anything to soothe their pain. My love for them was stronger than my hatred for the others.

This "easy" love saved me. This is where forgiveness starts.

* * *

I had another child. I knew he would be a boy, and that I would name him after my brother. Patou was born in Panama on January 19th, 1994.

Patrice had once jokingly told me that he wanted to be reincarnated as one of our children. My cousin Laure—who was close to Patrice—did not meet Patou until he was in his late teens. She told me that her heart stopped when she first saw him, because it was as if my brother was standing in front of her. His smile, his laugh, the way he moved and cocked his head, even the shape of his hands were my brother's.

2. A Good Life

Then, we give ourselves permission to live well.

For a while after Patrice's death, I would not let myself be happy. I felt guilty about any inkling of joy. How could I enjoy life when my brother did not get to live his, when my parents' world was shattered?

For two full years, I did not listen to music. I could not stand the emotions it evoked in me. I remember the first day I finally turned on the radio in the car in Panama and the Eagles' *Hotel California* came on. Finally, music did not hurt any longer.

We cannot forgive from a place of darkness, shut off from the joys of life.

We have to allow ourselves to feel the light on our face and the music in our heart.

> *Forgiveness is first for you, the forgiver... to release you from something that will eat you alive, that will destroy your joy and your ability to love fully and openly.*
> —W.M. Paul Young, *The Shack*

3. *Stop Being so Righteous*

We have to step off our pedestal to take that third step.

This is the hardest part.

Letting go always is.

I thought that letting go of my indignation meant I was giving up the fight, giving up on what was right. I was offended when my uncle Jeannot told me, just before my father's funeral: "Christine, you're hurting, but you have to realize that others are hurting too, in their own way." I was giving the eulogy and he was afraid of what I might say, specifically about the relatives that had abandoned my family.

I did not hear his words at the time. All I could hear was my own heart breaking all over again into sharp little shards of acute pain. How dare he compare our suffering with theirs? As always, words of wisdom do not echo wisdom until we are ready to hear them. I was not ready: I still needed my blanket of anger.

I admit I was tempted to be Edmond Dantès in that church pulpit, uttering words of recrimination in front of a captive audience. This would have been quite a coup. I could have been the preacher, the judge and the executioner. Isn't that what we are when we don't forgive?

I didn't do it because my children were there with me. I had worked hard to protect them from the family discord. Subconsciously, I also did not want to be vindictive in my grandmother's church. She would be heartbroken to see her family divided, and I knew that vengeful words would only make things worse. They always do.

Our grief does not entitle us to be righteous.

Being right does not entitle us to be righteous.

Most of my life, I had tried to "fix things," make them right. Expecting everyone to accept my judgment.

It did not work.

Righteousness is exhausting.

It does not solve anything.

It just perpetuates the cycle of pain.

4. *Let Go of Expectations*

You should never have expectations for other people, just be kind to them.

—Pema Chodron

Forgiving is rarely a big moment: tears flowing, violins playing in the background, fireworks lighting the skies. It just happens. Pema Chodron tells us: *My experience with forgiveness is that it comes spontaneously at a certain point and to try to force it is not really forgiveness.*

In an ideal world—my ideal world—those who had hurt us would have taken the first step, admitted how wrong they had been and begged us for forgiveness. On their knees.

But I had painstakingly learned to accept that they were going through their own *samsara*; they were stuck in their own cycle of suffering.

So, forgiveness just happened.

It flowed.

It healed.

Maman had forgiven first; it gave her peace.

As my uncle Bernard said: "We wasted so much time!"

But it was a lesson we all had to learn.

As we all gathered around Maman for her eightieth birthday last year, I looked around the room and felt infinite love and compassion for all these people that I had not been able to forgive for so long. I was finally free.

To forgive is to set a prisoner free and discover the prisoner was you.
—Lewis B. Smedes

THE 4 IMMEASURABLES

One of the most powerful and helpful of Patanjali's Yoga Sutras is Sutra I-33, also colorfully described as the *Four Locks, Four Keys* or *Catur Apramanah* in Buddhism:

By cultivating an attitude of friendship toward those who are happy, compassion toward those in distress, joy toward those who are virtuous, and equanimity toward those who are unvirtuous, lucidity arises in the mind.

To me, it describes the four stages of love, as we slowly expand the reaches of our heart from those who are easy to love to the unlovable.

The energy of love, given and received, cannot be quantified.

It is truly immeasurable.

As it grows, we grow.

1) *Maitri* or *Metta*: Loving-kindness for happy people.
2) *Karuna*: Compassion for those who suffer.
3) *Mudita*: Joy for others' happiness and success.
4) *Upeksha*: Equanimity, loving all beings the same, even the unlovable.

I realized that, for all those years, as I stumbled toward forgiveness, I was unknowingly following those precepts written thousands of years ago.

I had stumbled upon the truth, one clumsy step at a time.

I had to live my pain in order to find my truth.

I believed for so long that forgiving would be a betrayal of my love for my brother; I know now that I honor his memory every time I am forgiving and compassionate.

BASTILLE DAY 2016

Forgiveness is not an occasional act; it's a permanent attitude.

—Martin Luther King

I had just written the final words of this chapter when I heard of another deadly attack in my homeland in Nice. I thought that I had nicely wrapped up my story and its lesson, and could move on to the next chapter. But I should have known that the journey toward forgiveness never ends. As every lesson, it is not learned until it is lived.

Every single day.

Carolyn Myss states in *Anatomy of the Spirit* that our contemporary culture is stuck at the fourth chakra level, totally addicted to its wounds, focusing on the disease instead of the recovery. We let those wounds become our identity and use them as excuses for not moving forward.

We have to make the conscious decision to heal and, as all great spiritual teachers have taught us, the only way to heal is to forgive. It is probably one of the most difficult things we'll ever do, but it is the inescapable secret of Anahata and the key to spiritual liberation.

Our ability to genuinely connect to this central chakra through love, compassion and forgiveness will determine our ability to journey toward the three higher chakras and connect to our true divine nature. As we all learn to live lives of selfless service and value peace over war, we can help shake our society out of its fourth chakra status quo and lift it toward spiritual maturity.

The practice of forgiveness is our most important contribution to the healing of the world.

—Marianne Williamson

4. THE HEART CHAKRA: ANAHATA

COLOR: Green
TRANSLATION: Unstruck
LOCATION: Center of Chest
KEY WORDS: Unconditional Love, Compassion, Acceptance, Peace

RELATED BODY PARTS:
Heart, Breast, Circulatory System, Lungs, Arms, Hands, Shoulders, Ribs, Thoracic Spine, Diaphragm

QUALITIES WHEN BALANCED:
Open-heartedness, Trust, Gratitude, Compassion, Empathy, Kindness, Forgiveness, Generosity, Cheerfulness, Appreciation of Beauty, Unconditional Love, Balance

PSYCHOLOGICAL SIGNS OF IMBALANCE:
Depression, Anxiety, Loneliness and Isolation, Passivity, Fear of Closeness, Sadness, Hard-heartedness, Spite, Distrust, Bitterness, Taking for Granted, Self-righteousness, Ruthlessness, Self-Centeredness, Negativity, Inability to Love and Forgive, Resentment, Need for Vengeance

PHYSICAL SIGNS OF IMBALANCE:
Heart, Lung and Breathing Disorders (including Asthma), Breast Cancer, Chest Pain, Hypertension, Immune System Disorders

POSITIVE ARCHETYPE: The Lover   -
NEGATIVE ARCHETYPE: The Performer
ELEMENT: Air
SENSE: Touch
SOUND: YAM
VERB: I Love and I am Loved

FOOD: Leafy Vegetables

HEALING TOOLS

Self-study:

- Has your heart ever been broken?

- Are you afraid of getting hurt?

- Do you often feel lonely?

- Are there wounds that you have difficulty letting go of, that have become your identity?

- Is there anyone you have difficulty forgiving?

- Think of how the Four Immeasurables apply to your life.

Practical tools:

- Forgive yourself first
- Keep a Gratitude Journal: every night, write five things you were grateful for that day
- Gratitude or Happiness Jar: write one thing per day that made you happy or grateful and put it in the jar
- Write a letter to a loved one
- Write a letter to someone who is hurting
- Practice the 4 stages "From pain to forgiveness": Easy Love, A Good Life, Stop Being so Righteous, Let Go of Expectations
- Forgive someone on paper and release the forgiveness (burn the paper)
- Health grieving (counseling, group therapy, a good heart to heart talk with a friend)
- Surround yourself with people who love you unconditionally
- Love, give, donate, share
- Take loving care of someone or a pet
- Walk in nature, spend time in a flower garden and around greenery
- Wear green, display green objects and many green luscious plants
- Metta meditation: *May I be happy, May I be healthy, May I live with ease.* Then repeat the mantra thinking of a loved person, then a stranger, then someone who has hurt you, then ending with the whole world.
- Restorative Yoga: Reclining Butterfly (15 minutes), focusing on deep breathing and opening the heart fully
- Yin chest openers: Sphinx and Seal poses for several minutes
- Chant Mantra: OM MANI PADME HUM (The Jeweled Lotus: Sacred Tibetan chant supposed to embody the entire wisdom of the Buddha)

ASANAS: Back Bends/Chest Openers: Cobra, Sphinx, Locust, Camel, Upward-facing Dog; Triangle, Half Moon, Cow Face, Child, Fish

MANTRA: *I Am unconditionally Loving and unconditionally Loved*

HEART MEDITATION

Find a comfortable place where you feel safe and grounded
Sitting or lying down
Relaxing into the body and into the breath
Sending the breath to the heart center
The breath is a beautiful green glow that nourishes and warms your chest
Repeating your Mantra: *I Am unconditionally Loving and unconditionally Loved*
Starting to visualize yourself sitting around a campfire
Right in the middle of a clearing surrounded by lush verdant trees
You are in the heart of the forest
In its throbbing heart center
You feel the love of Mother Nature wrapping you in her warm embrace
I Am unconditionally Loved
Sitting by the fire, you start reciting the Metta prayer
May I be happy, May I be healthy, May I live with ease
Feeling unconditionally Loved
Feeling infinite compassion
Continuing the Metta Meditation thinking of someone in your life
May he/she be healthy, May he/she be happy, May he/she live with ease
As the invocation leaves your lips, seeing that person join you by the fire
In the heart of the forest
Feeling gratitude
Closing your eyes as you continue your Metta Meditation

One person at a time, the first person who comes to your mind
May he/she be healthy, May he/she be happy, May he/she live with ease
Until you need to open your eyes and look around you
At all the people who have joined you
Around the campfire
Feeling their love for you and your love for them
Feeling infinite gratitude and compassion
Knowing that they're unconditional
Now thinking of someone you need to forgive
May he/she be healthy, May he/she be happy, May he/she live with ease
Seeing that person join you by the fire
Feeling forgiveness
Feeling infinite gratitude and compassion
In the throbbing heartbeat of the forest
I Am unconditionally Loving and unconditionally Loved.

CHAPTER 5

VISHUDDHA THROAT CHAKRA

The thought manifests as the word

The thought manifests as the word;
The word manifests as the deed;
The deed develops into habit;
And habit hardens into character.
So watch the thought and its ways with care,
And let it spring from love
Born out of concern for all beings.

—Lao-Tzu or Buddha

Vishuddha is a powerful chakra: the way we express ourselves shapes our lives. Our innate purpose is to communicate our truth, to share the music within us. So why is it such a challenging task?

Because speaking our truth is not the easy path; it's uncomfortable. It singles us out and makes us different. It also tells the world who we really are. And the fear of being rejected is great. It is often easier to repeat someone else's words—someone who's already been endorsed by society—than to speak our own truth.

This is why it is so important to anchor ourselves into the solid ground of the first four chakras.

When we are firmly planted into our right to exist, to feel, to own our power, to love and to be loved, nothing is more natural than to speak our truth.

This is when we come into Vishuddha.

THOUGHTS

We are shaped by our thoughts; we become what we think.
When the mind is pure, joy follows like a shadow that never leaves.

—Buddha

In the past decades, there have been so many so-called self-help books, seminars and talk shows on the power of thoughts and intention that it's easy to disregard this principle as a New Age cliché. Just another gimmick to sell and make a profit. Another way to grab our attention. For $19.99, we can buy the book that will give us the secret to our authentic self. For a little more, we can order online the set of seven CDs that will direct our thoughts toward the right path. If we have the cash, we can also attend retreats in Hawaii or Costa Rica for a guaranteed life-changing experience.

I believe in the power of thoughts.

I believe that they create our reality.

But I don't believe that this is something you can buy or repeat like a parrot. There is no magic to it, just lots of discipline. And a hint of stubbornness.

Who could help me define the power of thoughts in the real world?

I decided to ask my children.

Why my children?

Because they are some of the most positive people I know and they seem to be very happy in the lives they have chosen for themselves.

John and I are not taking credit for it. We always told them that they could be and do whatever they dreamed of. This was very important to us, as we did not always have that support ourselves on our way into the world.

We did our best but we were definitely not perfect parents. There is no such super being anyway. As our youngest, Patou, told me with a twinkle in his eyes recently: "I've learned from you what NOT to do!" This is the way it should be; we pave the way for our children. They do have the advantage of centuries of trials and errors. Sometimes it takes a few generations to get it right. I am proud to say that they are indeed learning from all our mistakes.

So here are the wise words of my children:

Don't let your goals get in the way of your opportunities

Our daughter France-Lee has always been fiercely independent. She had the privilege of being our only child for six years before her first brother was born. I did everything with her; she was my little companion and I could see how she soaked everything in: from the French language to my organizing skills, her father's engineering ability and her grandmother's flair for cooking. This probably gave her two of her most amazing qualities: self-sufficiency and grounding into the certainty of who she is. When she was thirteen, she became a vegetarian before it became a trend. This was not easy, especially when she visited France—a country still firmly entrenched into a meat diet—and my family pestered her with concerns about her "unhealthy eating habits." She never wavered in her commitment to do what felt right for her, and is now a vegan.

She also has a wonderful ability to go with the flow of life. She has a vision, but is willing to surrender to whatever happens on her journey without fretting over it.

At thirty-one, she is living her dream. She lives in New York and Ireland with her Irish husband, works for Google and travels all over the world. She always knew this would be her life, and her thoughts directed her toward that path. She trusted that whatever opportunity was offered to her would be a stepping stone toward her goal. After a post-college sabbatical year in France, she spent a few months working at Starbucks in DC to make ends meet, then took her first job working in anti-piracy for the software entertainment industry. This prepared her for her current dream job, which came her way at a friend's wedding reception in Florida while conversing with one of the bridesmaids.

There is no wrong way to reach your dreams and, most of the time, the small side roads are a safer bet than the fast congested highways, where we miss so much. Letting ourselves take those small roads, letting ourselves surrender to the moment is often a better way to travel the journey of life.

Her philosophy mirrors an important yoga principle; *Vairagya* or non-attachment:

With constant remembrance of the Self, Vairagya, all yearnings fade.
—Sutra I-15

She is a shining example of a life lived well through surrender to our own true self and trust in whatever each moment brings.

Don't hit send

Our son JC has always been a charmer. When he was only a few months old, he would charm flight attendants and passengers. As a little boy, he would engage complete strangers in conversation. I'll never forget Labor Day 1999 at our Congressman's annual picnic in downtown Newport News. Then-President Clinton had made an appearance and was shaking hands after his speech. JC was right up front with his siblings and he announced clearly in his seven-year old voice: "You're my favorite best president ever." At twenty-five, he is still charming his way around a room and a crowd of people. He is very sensitive to the world around him and how that world responds to him and his actions. I think this gives him a strong sense of empathy, as he is very aware of others' feelings. He told me recently that he wants to make people happy. I was therefore not surprised when he told me of his life philosophy: "Whenever I have a strong reaction, I try to wait until the morning when my mind is clearer and not clouded by whatever feelings provoked that reaction. I might write it all down, let it out, but I don't hit send."

"Don't hit send" means that we don't make a rash decision we might regret, we don't act in anger, we don't "react." We put distance between us and the initial impulse. In our social media world, it consists of the actual physical act of not pushing a button on our phone, tablet or computer and releasing into the world that message we can never take back. It also means pausing before releasing that harsh word or gesture, pausing before making an important decision.

It means: take a moment.

It means: be aware.

It means: be mindful.

It is the essence of yoga, embodied in Sutra I-2, often described as the most important Sutra: *Yogas Chitta Vritti Nirodah.*

Chitta Vritti is the monkey mind, *Nirodah* is restraint.

Yoga is when we don't let ourselves be controlled by our monkey mind. When we don't attach ourselves to our thoughts and emotions as they erratically jump from branch to branch.

Yoga is when we don't hit send.

Don't share your intentions with too many people, or they will lose their potency.

Patou, our youngest is the most grounded of our three children. Perhaps because he had the advantage of learning from his siblings' mishaps. But most certainly because years playing kicker on his high school and college teams taught him to be steady and dependable.

He has planned his life just as he prepared for his football kicks—calmly preparing the perfect spot for the ball, stepping back into position unruffled by the brouhaha of the stadium, pausing and, only when he was ready, giving the signal for the run and the awaited kick. My chest would squeeze itself into a tight knot of worry and I would often be afraid to look, in case the ball would not make it over the goal post. Whichever happened, Patou would stay composed as he jogged back to the sideline.

After college, he got his first interview, which led to his first job in Lynchburg, three hours away from our home. Before we knew it, he had found a lovely apartment and was moving there. He was starting his brand-new life without any fuss or drama.

He had a plan all along, since he discovered his love for water treatment in a biology project and had worked toward it. Slow and steadfast.

His philosophy: "As humans, it's innate for us to strive toward something better and something more. Oftentimes when we are in a stagnant state, we feel as if we have to express our goals to those surrounding us. The only problem with this is that we are receiving the satisfaction from their response which, in turn, lets us subconsciously feel as if it has already happened. Be wary of why and whom you tell because those personal endeavors are more powerful when they are closer to you, with only you knowing and understanding."

In a nutshell, if you talk too much about your goals, you've already achieved some satisfaction from that sharing and you don't strive as much to accomplish them.

This struck a chord with me, as I have been saying my whole life that I am a writer. Somehow saying it robbed me of the effort of "being it." This time, as I am laboring on this book, I have not shared as much and kept this project closer to my heart.

This reminds me of the yoga principle of *Abhyasa:*

*Devoted practice is nurtured by a sustained, steady rhythm and a
dedicated heart.*

—Sutra I-14

Discipline is a private endeavor that doesn't need advertising, just
commitment.

WORDS

*I know nothing in the world that has as much power as a word.
Sometimes I write one, and I look at it, until it begins to shine.*

—Emily Dickinson

I work with words. I know the power of words.

As a translator, I've learned the nuances of a language that can only
be felt with the heart. Words are alive and should be treated as such.

Words have a vibration and a cadence that affect us emotionally
and spiritually.

Some of them cannot be translated: their essence cannot be
reproduced in any other language.

In French, *coquin* means playful, mischievous and cute all rolled into
one unique word that makes one smile. A *câlin* is softer and longer than
a hug, it's an embrace that goes beyond the physical; you don't give
câlins to just anybody, you abandon yourself to a *câlin,* as a giver and a
receiver.

In Spanish, *la sobremesa* is that leisurely time spent "on the table"
after lunch or dinner, talking and enjoying each other's company.

In German, *gemütlich* sounds just like its cozy, warm, friendly
meaning. Like a comfortable chair one just wants to sink in with a
satisfied sigh.

In Norwegian, *hyggelig* means just plain nice and right and content.
Just saying the word makes one happy!

In Sanskrit, the language of yoga, the sound of *Om* is the sound of the universe. As it vibrates and lingers through one's whole being, it heals. It connects.

As I sit in Buddhist meditation halls, I chant Pali words without needing to know their meaning. Their music throbs deep within me. It speaks to me. It connects me to their universal meaning.

Words are felt in the heart before they are heard in the mind.

We should be careful with our words.

Their echo remains long after they have been spoken.

Words should be bridges, not walls.

In my profession, I have always been extremely cautious about the nuance and impact of a translated word. I try to convey its intrinsic meaning rather than the lexicon version. I have unfortunately not always been so careful in my personal life.

The 2016 American presidential elections shook me to my core and, like so many others, my words rode recklessly on the back of my emotions. Yes, I am allowed my opinions, just as everyone else is. The amazing freedom we experience in our society is rooted in the meshing of our differences, just as the most breathtaking part of any day is that time when day blends into night and night into day. We have the right and the responsibility to express our views. But we also have the responsibility to use words that unite instead of divide. We should not regret expressing our voice, but we might regret the words used in the heat of the moment.

This challenging time has been a lesson in two important yoga principles: the two *Niyamas Ahimsa* (no-harm) and *Satya* (telling the truth). Those two are intrinsically linked and the ultimate decision is ours. Can we speak our truth without causing any harm? Or is the truth more important, even if it causes harm?

It all comes back to our intention: whether to tell the truth for the good of all or to satisfy the ego.

Is our truth pure or just a pretext to agitate and possibly cause harm?

Ultimately, we should speak our truth when we trust that it benefits the greater good and that keeping quiet is more detrimental than speaking up.

Before using our words, simply asking ourselves: "Do I want to be right or do I want to be kind?" is all we need to make the right decision.

* * *

The following story exemplifies the perilous power of words:

Le Corbeau

Growing up, I would hear adults speak of *Le Corbeau*.

There would be outrage and a hint of fear in their voices.

They would tell stories of unspeakable evil caused by *Le Corbeau*. This mythical raven would drop anonymous letters in mailboxes— vicious missives that would create havoc. As a child, I imagined a huge ominous black bird carrying letters in its beak and dropping them in every villager's mailbox before flying back to its cave in the depths of hell.

These poison-pen letters would reveal secrets, start rumors, defame characters and ruin lives. The subjects ranged from adultery, questioning paternity of children, to accusations of dishonesty and hypocrisy, such as misappropriating funds from town councils and committees.

The term was coined in a 1943 Henri-Georges Clouzot movie of the same title during the German Occupation, a period rife with betrayals and secret denunciations, and it became the common term for a malicious informant. Maman remembers those letters well, as their salacious content spread throughout the village. She tells me that some of those accusations were vicious lies but some were indeed true.

* * *

So, wasn't *Le Corbeau* doing a public service by denouncing the shady deeds going on under the villagers' noses? Shouldn't he have been acclaimed instead of vilified?

My answer is: What was his intention?

The person who called himself *Le Corbeau* used words to cause harm, too cowardly to sign his own name. When we speak the truth, we do it in the light, with the full integrity of our name out in the open. If *Le Corbeau*'s true goal was justice, he would have made his revelations through the proper channels, trying to cause as little harm as possible.

Some misdeeds needed to be told, especially if they hurt the villagers' interests or well-being. But we have to know why we speak up; are we doing it out of ego, anger, malevolence, retribution or to help?

Words should be used to tell the truth, but only a shining truth, not a truth delivered under the cover of darkness carried under the black wings of a raven. As Swami Vivekananda tells us: *If in doubt whether to observe Ahimsa or Satya, always go with Ahimsa.*

DEEDS

Don't ask what the world needs. Ask what makes you come alive and go do it. Because what the world needs is people who have come alive.
—Howard Thurman

When I was twenty-one and studying in Munich in 1982, I lived for a few months with a formidable woman, Ursula Redepenning.

In 1970 at only age twenty-six, she had been the youngest elected representative to the Bayerische Landtag (Bavarian parliament) for the FDP, the German Democratic Party. She was running for elections again that fall of 1982 and did not have much hope; her party was not doing well.

She was divorced; her husband had not been able to handle her success and had left her for his secretary. I was staying with her as an au pair to help with her two teenage children. Now in her late thirties, she was at one of the crossroads in her life, with major changes for the country and her career if the FDP lost the elections.

We spent long evenings talking—or rather I listened to her talk—about her life and what she had learned along the way, while sipping wine. Red for her, white for me. I was impressed by her, not by her success, but by the deep commitment that drove her life. She was not into appearances and status symbols; she was into meaning. She had entered politics in order to make a difference and help those who had not been as fortunate as she had been. She was powerful but she was kind; she was highly intelligent but never condescending.

One evening, our conversation lingered late into the night, and she told me of a trip to India where she had been confronted by the immense poverty of that country. Of course, she had heard about it, but experiencing it firsthand had overwhelmed her to the point of nausea. She had felt shame that there could be such poverty. She had felt disgust for governments that could let this happen with impunity. She had promised herself to do everything in her power to fight for those people everyone forgot so easily. And then, she said something I will never forget: "Most of my life I've done everything I was expected to do. I love my children more than anything and I cannot imagine my life without them but, if I had to do it again, I would not have children. There are so many other children in the world I could help if I didn't have my own. There is so much more I could do to help the world. In a way, having children was a selfish act on my part."

She was a fantastic mother, one of the best I had ever seen in my years as an au pair. I myself benefited from her nurturing spirit as I joined the family for daily home-cooked meals, fun outings to the Tiergarten, the museum or the Beerfest, as well as trips to the Alps at a Bavarian farm. What she said did not shock me; it made sense. She knew her calling, and she did not apologize for it any longer. She had tried to please everyone by being the perfect young woman, smart and pretty, exemplary wife and mother, popular political prodigy. She had realized that this image did not really fit who she was. She seemed old to me at the time because I was so young, but she was only in her late thirties and I'm pretty sure she followed her path as soon as her children were grown.

I wish she knew how much she has helped me trust myself.

Her voice has echoed in my mind throughout my life—this voice that doesn't apologize when speaking its innermost truth.

Before we went to bed that night, she leaned toward me and said softly: "Don't ever apologize for being who you are; don't belittle yourself, your intelligence or your beliefs to make others feel better. Be who you want to be. Do what you really need to do."

THE SNAKE WHISTLE

During a recent trip to Peru, John and I spent time in the Amazon. We stayed in a lodge nestled between jungle and river, only accessible by canoe.

The first thing I saw when I entered our private lodge was a whistle on a lanyard hanging from a hook. The snake whistle. I had heard about it, but seeing it was another story.

It really existed.

It was there for a reason.

The reason was that there might be snakes in our room.

This didn't reassure me. This whistle seemed to represent all my hidden fears.

During dinner, I talked to our guide and some of the attendants about the whistle. They all smiled, even laughed, and told me that the whistle was rarely used to report a snake. Guests had blown the whistle to report small bugs, or even nothing at all. The whistle was just there to make them feel better, to give them a tool to express their fears and ask for help.

Returning to our cabin, I looked at the whistle differently, as a friend instead of a frightening object. It represented my voice. An opportunity to be heard, whatever the circumstances. It was okay to grab the whistle and blow, but we could not abuse it. Because who listens any longer when a whistle blows non-stop?

We all have a snake whistle within, a voice that begs to be heard. Just like the snake whistle, that voice scares us. Will anyone hear? What if no one comes? What will people think? Will it sound funny? Or stupid? Do I have the right to blow the whistle? It's here, hanging on the hook, but am I allowed?

Yes, it is our duty to blow that whistle, to express ourselves in spite of fears.

And just like the whistle, fears dissipate as soon as we've made that sound.

As we blow the snake whistle, we regain our innate power and allow our voice to be heard.

That voice that begs to be heard.

You can't find your voice if you don't use it.

—Austin Kleon

5. THE THROAT CHAKRA: VISHUDDHA

COLOR: Blue
SANSKRIT TRANSLATION: Purification
LOCATION: Throat
KEY WORDS: Communication, Self-Expression, Creativity, Free Will

RELATED BODY PARTS: Throat, Ears, Nose, Teeth, Mouth, Neck, Tongue, Shoulders, Arms, Hands

QUALITIES WHEN BALANCED:
Speaking our Truth, Non-Attachment, Patience, Faith, Loyalty, Trust, Devotion, Organization and Planning, Inner Silence

PSYCHOLOGICAL SIGNS OF IMBALANCE:
Communication Problems, Attachment, Impatience, Being Manipulative, Cynicism, Lack of Devotion and Self-Knowledge, Shyness, Blocked Creativity, Mood Swings, Difficulty Maintaining a Spiritual Path and Choosing a Vocation, Samsara: Feeling stuck in the Wheel of Life (Conditioning and Ego)

PHYSICAL SIGNS OF IMBALANCE:
Weak Voice, Speech Defect, Thyroid Imbalance, Swollen Glands, Hearing Problems, Stiff Neck, Sore Throat, Metabolic Disorders, Colds, Flu and Fevers

POSITIVE ARCHETYPE: The Communicator
NEGATIVE ARCHETYPE: The Silent Child
ELEMENT: Space
SENSE: Hearing
SOUND: HAM
VERB: I Express Myself
FOOD: Fasting (juices)

HEALING TOOLS

Self-study:

- What powerful thoughts guide you?

- Do you feel the power of words in your life?

- Can you remember instances when you had to choose between Ahimsa (non-harming) and Satya (truth)?

- Have you encountered *Le Corbeau* in your life?

- What actions make you feel alive?

- How do you want to use your Voice?

- What is your snake whistle?

Practical tools:

- Write down your most positive and uplifting thoughts
- Whenever you have a negative dark thought, replace it with a positive thought
- Write a journal, tell or write stories, poetry
- Immerse yourself in Art
- Sing, chant, hum, scream
- Play drums
- Read, recite poetry—aloud if possible
- Read, listen to or learn a new language
- Develop the ability to express your own opinions—political or others—in a non-confrontational manner
- Meaningful conversations
- Listen to the sounds of nature
- Wear blue and surround yourself with blue objects, linen or flowers
- Be in silence: Mauna
- Recite Mantras
- Bija Mantras (Seed sounds for each Chakra): LAM VAM RAM YAM HAM OM

ASANAS: Neck and Shoulder Rolls and Shrugs, Knee to Ear, Camel, Forward Bends, Legs up the Wall, Fish

MANTRA: *I Speak in my Own Voice*

THROAT CHAKRA MEDITATION

Find a comfortable place where you feel safe and grounded
Sitting or lying down
Relaxing into the body and into the breath
Sending the breath to the throat
The breath is a beautiful blue glow that nourishes and warms your
    throat
Repeating your Mantra: *I Speak in my Own Voice*
Starting to visualize yourself standing in the middle of a busy street
In the midst of a very busy city
In the midst of a very busy world
Noise all around you
Everyone talking, yelling, car horns blaring, traffic roaring, sirens
Everyone, everything vying for attention
What about you?
You want to be heard
I Speak in my Own Voice
Opening your mouth, trying to speak
No sound coming out
You have lost your voice
Despair
Frantically making your way through the crowd
Everyone pushing everyone
Down the busy street
Arriving at the end of the street in front of a gate
Looking behind you at the cacophony of noises and people
Opening the gate
Closing it behind you
Shutting away all the noises
Turning around
You are standing in silence
You are in the most beautiful garden you have ever seen

It is vibrant with colorful flowers and trees
Branches and leaves rustling in the gentle wind
And birds, chirping melodically
Their song a part of the silence
You sit on a bench
In the center of this exquisite haven
You absorb the silence and the sounds of Nature
When you open your eyes, you see a stone well and walk toward it
There is a cup on its ledge
You dip it into the clear water and bring it to your lips
Feeling the cool refreshing water trickling down your throat
Healing
I Speak in my Own Voice
You take a deep breath in
And exhale into the most magical sound of Om you have ever heard
I Speak in my Own Voice
You start chanting, singing and dancing, expressing all that you are
Expressing all your creative gifts
In the beautiful garden
I Speak in my Own Voice.

CHAPTER 6

AJNA CHAKRA
THIRD EYE

Trust your intuition

We don't receive wisdom; we must discover it for ourselves after a journey that no one can take from us or spare us from.

—Marcel Proust

Ajna chakra is the gateway into the world of our soul. Our two physical eyes allow us to see the outside world, but our third eye gives us the ability to see the unseen and know the unknown. Think of it as an inner light that illuminates everything we have always wanted to know and gives us access to supreme Consciousness. Our vision knows no boundaries, it can explore and benefit from all that is, has ever been, and ever will be.

Once again, it is very important to be grounded before we open that gate. We will undoubtedly know if we are; the light will not blind us but bring clarity to everything. That clarity does not take us away from our lives but allows us to live more fully. Because we can see our path very clearly. And with this comes a sense of great peace.

We come into the gift of Ajna chakra with great patience and mindfulness.

This is a vision that requires us to close our eyes and be still.

GREEN LIGHT, RED LIGHT

Yoga is a mirror to look at ourselves from within.

—B.K.S. Iyengar

When I started practicing yoga, I discovered its partner, its soul sister: meditation.

I understood the concept but understanding didn't make doing easier.

I read the required books and tried different techniques.

I asked some of my teachers and fellow students for advice. They talked about Transcendental Meditation, candle gazing, and breath counting, but when I asked about their own practice, their answers were vague. I realized most of them were as clueless as I was.

My personal practice was a struggle. A torture. I dreaded it.

As soon as I sat down, it was open season on my mind. A flood of unwelcome thoughts rushed in, pulling me into all different directions. My most current worries arrived first, followed by more ancient repressed feelings I had thought were long forgotten. My monkey mind—that relentless flow of thoughts jumping from one branch to another like a monkey—was on steroids, on spring break. Monkeys gone wild! I didn't know how to stop this onslaught. I just wanted to sit down and connect with my higher self but I was confronted by turmoil and petty thoughts.

I knew that yoga without meditation was just stretching.

Pleasant but just an empty physical exercise.

Calming the mind is yoga. Not just standing on the head.

—Swami Satchidananda

I felt deep in my gut how important yoga was and would continue to be in my life, and I didn't want to stop at the threshold of this mystical journey. As Elizabeth Gilbert said: *Meditation is both the anchor and the wings of yoga. Meditation is the way.*

So, I persisted.

But how could I hope to embody the essence of something so challenging?

I felt like a meditation hypocrite, praising the practice but unable to find any satisfaction in it myself.

I was looking for some magical formula that would allow me to sit in a perfect lotus position with a knowing Buddha smile on my lips.

But sitting still didn't come easy to me.

And then, one day, I had a revelation: when your kitchen sink leaks, you don't try to fix it yourself; you call a professional.

My mind was leaking. I needed to go to the meditation professionals.

The Buddhist monks.

I had heard of the Thai Buddhist temple across the James River Bridge, thirty minutes from my house. I knew they had a special meditation session for English speakers every Wednesday night, but had never felt any need to go. Until now.

The drive itself on that late summer afternoon was a metaphor: my friend Del and I were crossing the bridge into a place of peace and serenity.

The temple—Wat Pasantidhamma—was an exotic splash of color nestled in the Virginia woods.

The orange-clad monks welcomed us with a smile.

No fuss. No formula. No gimmick.

They told us to just sit.

And we sat.

Facing the back of the monks and the golden statues of the smiling Buddha surrounded by an array of flowers.

We sat for thirty minutes while they chanted.

We sat for thirty more minutes in silence.

We did walking meditation for thirty minutes.

We sat again for fifteen minutes.

When I stood up, I knew my life had changed forever; I felt brand new, as if I had taken a shower from the inside.

Monkey mind had come as always. But this time, after my first usual instinct to fight it, I had let go and just observed its senseless little dance. Without the momentum of my resistance, it seemed to have slowly given up. The waves of unrest had become just ripples. And between those ripples, I had caught a glimpse of glorious peace, as someone catches glimpses of sun when the storm starts to abate. Those glimpses were all I needed to gain hope and continue to sit.

Meditation is a surrender. It's not a demand. It's not forcing existence your way. It is relaxing into the way existence wants you to be. It is a let-go.

—Osho

I didn't need books, techniques or advice. I needed surrender, reverence and simplicity.

I didn't need someone to tell me, I needed someone to show me.

That day, I met my teacher, my friend: Ajahn Piya. His name means beloved. And no other name could fit him better.

Over the next two years, he showed us and taught us the essence of Theravada (traditional Buddhism) and its golden child: Vipassana (insight meditation).

Every Wednesday evening, after our two hours of meditation, we would sit down for Dhamma talk: a one-hour lesson.

He taught us patience, discipline, and wisdom wrapped in kindness and compassion.

He taught us that, just as a boxer practices every day for his big match, we train our mind to prepare for the challenges of life. Whenever challenges arise, we're ready to handle them.

Meditation is like a gym in which you develop the powerful mental muscles of calm and insight.

—Ajahn Brahm

He taught us that struggling was normal, some days more than others, but we had to be patient and just sit, knowing it was good for us.

I like to tell people who don't understand the point of meditation that, just as we need to clean our house regularly, we need to clean our mind. First, when we sit, all we see is dust. As we start cleaning, the dust flies everywhere and you see more dust and cobwebs in the corners, under the furniture, and there seems to be no end to it. It can get overwhelming and you just want to give up. But if you persevere, your house and your mind start becoming cleaner, clearer. No more cobwebs in the corners of your house and the corners of your mind, just tidiness. And peace.

And the more often you do it, the less time it takes to dust. Cobwebs and dust balls don't have time to grow out of control.

I meditate so that I can inundate my entire being with the omnipotent power of peace.

—Sri Chinmoy

Ajhan Piya once asked us what traffic light we preferred. Everyone said green, because we all have places to go, important things to do, and sitting at a red light is a waste of time.

He said: "I understand that you're all busy and no one likes to stop at a red light, but what would happen if everyone had the green light? If everyone could go non-stop all the time? It would not work. It would cause big traffic accidents. It's the same for your lives; when you have the green light all the time and never stop, it doesn't work. Accidents are going to happen. Illness, stress and unhappiness will happen. Meditation is your red light. When it comes, welcome it. Enjoy that break, that moment of stillness, of non-doing. You need the red light in your life as much as you need the green light."

I have used that metaphor many times in my life when I've been confronted with a red light. It made me realize each time that there was a reason for this obstacle in the road; a lesson or a wink from the universe telling me I needed a break, I needed to pause and think. Recalculate.

I am grateful for the red lights in my life.

For the pauses.

As my practice deepened, I started thinking about the other light—the amber light—and the difficult choice it gives us: should we stop or should we go?

We have no idea when the light will change, in traffic or in our lives.

Will we be prepared to make that decision? Is it safer to stop or just keep going?

Some of us are afraid of the amber light and the choice it gives us, especially when we have been hurt at a crossroad of life.

I understood that that light was the culmination of our practice. Meditation taken into the world.

Our ability to make the right decisions we face in life.

Anchored in our practice, we instinctively know what to do.

The amber light is Intuition.

The soul always knows what to do to heal itself. The challenge is to silence the mind.

—Caroline Myss

THE ROAD IN THE DARK WOODS

The power of intuitive understanding will protect you from harm until the end of your days.

—Lao Tzu

As a child, I spent a lot of time by myself or by silently observing the world around me, and I think this helped me develop my intuition.

The next step was to trust that intuition.

The spring of my eleventh birthday, my family moved from the town of Lagnieu to our brand-new house in my grandparents' village, Leyment, five miles away.

I had been taking a bus every weekday from Lagnieu to my private middle school in the next town, Ambérieu. After the move, since only a few months of school remained, my parents decided to let me use the same bus, with the help of my uncle Georges.

Georges worked at the glass factory, Saint-Gobain, just at the entrance of Lagnieu, and I started riding with him to the school bus stop (right by the factory) every morning. In the afternoon, the bus would drop me off at the same stop, at around 5:30 pm, where I would wait for my uncle (usually outside of his office). He would drive me back to Leyment around 6 pm. It involved some waiting time for me, but back then adults were not at the service of children; adults' time had priority. I was excited about the new house and didn't mind the arrangement which allowed me to have more time with my bus friends.

One afternoon—strangely I forgot the reason why—our bus left school one hour late. As the minutes passed by, anxiety started to take hold of me. We were going to be late. Georges would be upset. Or perhaps he would leave without me. I quickly rejected that idea: how could he do that? Playing the different scenarios in my mind, I decided that, if I didn't see his car, I would ask my friend Catherine to go to her house.

When the bus stopped by Saint-Gobain, after 7 pm, I could see the parking lot was almost empty, and I hesitated. I didn't want to be that weak girl who asks for help. And anyway, Georges was certainly waiting for me in his office or in the parking lot. He would be so upset if I went to someone's house. Moreover, Catherine's parents would be inconvenienced to have to drive me home. Remember, this was a time when we had not only no cell phones, but also no home phones. We would not get one until 1976 when I was fifteen. There were not many options. With a heavy heart, I got off the bus.

Thinking of that young girl, adjusting her heavy backpack, standing alone by the road at the edge of that deserted factory in the late afternoon, watching the bus—and with it the safety it represented—disappear, brings tears to my eyes.

As soon as the bus left, my instinct was screaming that I had made a mistake. I perused the parking lot; Georges' car was not there. Beyond hope, I walked to the factory gates; they were closed. Two choices remained: walk to my friend's house in town and ask for help or walk the longer distance to my village, five miles away, up Le Charveyron hill and through a long stretch of woods that opened up into Leyment. The first choice seemed safest but, again, out of fear and pride, I didn't trust my instinct and I decided to walk home. Anyway, Georges had obviously told my parents I wasn't at the bus stop and they were on their way to pick me up. I would meet them on the road. How could they not be worried about me?

I started walking through the house subdivision at the edge of Lagnieu.

After almost one mile, I started climbing Le Charveyron, lined with the small cluster of houses that made up the hamlet. My parents had lived there their first year of marriage. Maman had told me that there was no indoor bathroom, no comfort, but it was their own place. She also said this was where Papa had started to change and treat her poorly. Selfishly, he drove their moped to work and let her use the bicycle to climb up the hill to her workplace, the hill I was climbing now.

My backpack felt heavier and my breath became labored as I trudged up the steep incline. My heart was also feeling heavy. Few cars had passed me since I had started walking. None were my parents' car. As I neared the last houses of the hamlet, a short straight deserted stretch of road awaited me, before the sharp left turn into the dark woods.

I would have to walk two miles through the woods.

The sun was setting. That ominous time between day and night was taking over the landscape, creating shadows where there had been none before.

By the time I entered the woods, night would have taken over.

Perhaps it would be for the best. In darkness, I could hide my terror, shame and tears.

I passed the last house and followed the road between the fields.

What other choice did I have but to keep walking?

My body was in full alert: sweaty skin, tight belly, pounding chest, wobbly legs.

Red light. Red light.

A car passed me—I tried to make myself invisible by lowering my head to my chest.

It stopped a few feet in front of me, and waited.

I stopped also, immobilized by fear.

The hamlet was behind me and ahead was the turn into the forest.

I was alone.

Completely alone.

Should I run into the fields?

Run where?

I was so tired. My backpack was so heavy.

The car started to slowly back up until it was level with me. The driver, a man of my parents' age, lowered the passenger window and called out to me. I tried to ignore him but he insisted: "Bonsoir. What are you doing walking by yourself so late? Do you need a ride?"

I took a few steps, choking back the tears: "No I'm fine. I'm just walking home. It's not far."

His tone was incredulous: "Are you sure? Where are you going?"

"Home. And my parents are on their way to pick me up."

Why didn't he just go away?

"Wait a minute, are you Thérèse's girl? I know your mother."

I slowed down, relenting a little, but still in survival mode. That's what those bad men did, trying to have you trust them before they abducted you: "I'm fine, I can walk."

"I really know her. I'm Monsieur Plumeau, the plumber. I live in Leyment too. You can't walk to Leyment by yourself so late. It's too far."

I wanted to believe him; he knew my family and I had heard of him.

Amber light.

I had to make a decision, fast. I almost felt as if my life depended on it.

Choosing between the danger he represented or—what I felt in my gut—the greater one lurking in the woods.

The fear of the dark woods was unbearable. I could either walk through them or drive through them in the safety of his car. I relented: "I've been told not to ride with strangers, but you know my family, so I guess that's okay."

He smiled and opened the passenger door.

I sat as far away from him as I could, leaning against the window, ready to escape if I needed to.

We drove to the intersection and turned left into the woods.

As we entered the darkness, we saw an old grey van parked on the side of the road, right by one of the paths leading into the depth of the forest. Five or six men were huddled beside it. I didn't know what they were doing, I didn't care. All I could see in my mind's eye was a little schoolgirl, carrying a heavy backpack, entering the dark deserted road into the woods, and seeing those men, and those men seeing her. Night falling.

From the corner of my eye, I saw Monsieur Plumeau look at me and shake his head.

When he dropped me off, I wanted to say: "Thank you for saving me." But all I said was "Merci."

I never told my story.

Because no one had missed me.

My parents were so involved with their own lives that they had not realized my uncle had not picked me up and that I should have been home hours earlier. My mother later mentioned something about Georges being upset because he had to wait five minutes for me and then decided to drive home without me, but neither of them seemed concerned about how I'd found my way home. I think I mentioned walking and being picked up by Monsieur Plumeau. She replied: "Oh, yes, he's a nice man."

From then on, I believed in my intuition.

I knew this was all I could rely on, because people—even our loved ones—often failed us.

Every time life led me to the edge of dark woods, I stopped, considered the alternatives and chose the route that led me away from danger.

I trust my intuition. And it rarely fails me.

Intuition is a spiritual faculty. It does not explain, but simply points the way.

—Florence Scovel Shinn

SPIRITUAL QUEST

The spiritual life doesn't remove us from the world, but leads us deeper into it.

—Henry J.M. Nouwen

Exploring a spiritual quest seems somewhat self-involved when half the planet is on a quest for survival, looking for food and shelter while some of us are looking for the meaning of life.

But finding our spirit and our purpose helps the world.

When we connect to our intention, all of our actions become relevant.

"We are spiritual beings, having a human experience" is a common phrase. But being human is a full-time job, especially in our young adult years. We are told that we need to find a job, a home, a mate, procreate and spend the remaining time maintaining everything we have acquired. Later on, when our chain of obligations settles and our nest empties, we have more time to dwell on our spiritual essence.

The 4 Stages

In Hinduism, the stages of life are clearly defined as *Ashramas*, and follow a very natural pattern of our human and spiritual evolution:

- *Brahmacharya* (Student): time for gaining knowledge through play, studies and introspection.
- *Grihastha* (Householder): time to explore the duties and pleasures of the world, working, mating and raising a family.
- *Vanaprastah* (Forest Dweller or Retiree)): time to take an advisory role, in work and family, and have more leisure to focus on spiritual matters.
- *Sannyasa* (Renouncer): time to let go of ties to the material world and focus on service and liberation through spirit.

Our spiritual journey seems to bookend our existence. But one who is ready and so inclined can dedicate her entire life to the spiritual and go straight from being the Student to being the Renouncer, as do our most revered spiritual leaders.

Stage 1: The Student

As a child, I think I would have been happy living in a monastery: I loved to read, study and be by myself. But I also dreamed of traveling the world speaking different languages and experiencing new cultures, so being a nun didn't seem like a lasting vocation for me, unless I could be a traveling nun. All I knew was that I had a deep longing for something intangible and my times alone helped me toward it.

In my world—which was very limited—spirituality was Catholicism. Period. The true, one and only religion. I was not exposed to other religions, even less yoga, Buddhism or meditation. We studied other cultures in school, but as something foreign and exotic. Even Protestantism was an abomination. The first time I went abroad to England, I did not dare attend an Anglican service, afraid it would taint my innocent Catholic soul.

My early spiritual journey was an exploration of the written word. My cravings for substance seemed appeased only when I read the great poets and writers. The more tormented they were, the more they spoke to my soul. Through them, I learned that I was not alone in my elusive quest for something that didn't have a name. They were my ancestors, my guides. I loved the *Poëtes Maudits* (the Cursed Poets): Baudelaire, Verlaine and Rimbaud. But I also admired the wisdom of Rousseau and Voltaire and the genius of Victor Hugo. I am grateful for all my French literature and philosophy teachers who encouraged my search for meaning in the works of those great authors, as well as my passion for the written word. As I furthered my studies, learning new languages was just an opportunity to throw myself into the original texts of my favorite writers: Keats, Byron, Pablo Neruda, Goethe, Herman Hesse…

The words of Herman Hesse guided me through my college years. There were others, but at this stage of my life, his *Steppenwolf* touched me like no other book. Similarly to his hero, I felt like *that beast astray who finds neither joy nor home nor nourishment in a world that is strange and incomprehensible to him.*

Man is nothing else than the narrow and perilous bridge between nature and spirit. His innermost destiny drives him on to the spirit and to God. His innermost longing draws him back to nature, and the mother. Between the two forces his life hangs tremulous and resolute.

Like so many teenagers, my early spiritual quest was self-involved, fraught with angst and passion. More despair than joy. I was learning all the right notes, but needed the experience of real life to be able to make my spirit dance.

I thought being spiritual meant you didn't belong in the world.

I had to learn that spirit is the ease of being yourself in the world.

I needed to be a Householder.

The deity is within you, not in ideas and books. Truth is lived, not taught.

—Herman Hesse, *The Glass Bead Game*

Stage 2: The Householder

Being a Householder gave my soul roots. It softened and molded it into the warmth of the earth. It gave it substance and context.

My spiritual journey became more settled as I experienced the duties and joys of the world. Being an active part of society with jobs and responsibilities, finding a loving life partner with whom I created and nurtured a family, discovering the meaning of love and loss, gave my soul texture.

It helped me build the nurturing foundation in which my spirit could blossom.

A spiritual quest is always a step forward from a place of love; it's an embrace, not a rejection.

"The seat of the soul is where the inner and the outer world meet."

—Joseph Campbell

Stage 3: The Forest-Dweller

Centuries ago, seekers literally went to live in the forest, as a symbol of their detachment from the material world. After my father died and France-Lee graduated from high school, I needed to spend more time in the forest, to devote more time to my spiritual studies.

John and I had joined our neighborhood Methodist church when we moved to Virginia. We had bought our first house and we wanted to give our children a sense of community and the Methodist faith seemed a good middle ground between my Catholic upbringing and other Protestant creeds. Moreover, John's uncle was a Methodist minister and I liked his pragmatism. Honestly, I was overwhelmed with the multitude of different churches just in our town. I had been taught that the Christian faith was divided in two: Catholics and Protestants. I was realizing that this was just the tip of the religious iceberg. Americans loved variety in their faiths as they did in their supermarkets. I did not comprehend the differences but was willing to learn. Our church community was welcoming and loving. I taught Sunday school for six years, our children attended youth services and sang in the choir, and I learned the subtle differences between Catholicism and the other Christian faiths. I loved the service aspect of our church, but I came to realize that I missed the mysticism of my childhood faith. I thought Protestantism would help me to integrate religion into my life. It did, but I realized religion was not what I needed; I craved spirituality.

So, I embarked on my spiritual journey.

I had a traveling companion, a friend from our Methodist church. We recognized our common thirst for a spiritual journey almost instantly. In the words of Elizabeth Lesser; we wanted *to put our souls in charge of our lives, but we didn't know how.* So, we decided to learn together.

The details of our exploration don't matter. A spiritual journey is not a "one size fits all." There is no generic itinerary into your soul. No one can tell you what to do, where to go, what to read or study; you have to discover and follow your own path. When *Eat Pray Love* became an international phenomenon in the nineties, it struck a chord in millions of women who, just like the author Elizabeth Gilbert, realized how empty their lives were. But instead of following their own path, they replicated her exact geographical journey: Italy, India and Bali, expecting to achieve the same awakening and, why not, find a Brazilian husband in the process. Gilbert lamented that they had missed the point; a soul journey is the most intimate and vulnerable journey you will ever take and it is not something you can copy and paste into your life. It is unpredictable. A step into Mystery.

We can help and support each other, but we cannot walk each other's path.

My friend and I started our quest with a desire to deepen our knowledge of our own Christian faith. This led us to discover the difference between the dark side of each religion: artificial, dogmatic, man-made and power-hungry, and its true essence of love, tolerance and compassion. As we studied other religions, we realized they all share that true essence. Underneath the pomp and dogma beats the same divine heart.

I belong to no religion. My religion is Love. Every heart is my temple.
—Rumi

We traveled the same roads but found a different purpose. She returned to the Catholic faith of her youth with a deeper commitment. I found myself drawn to Eastern philosophy and I knew I had arrived home when I discovered yoga. I had been looking for a spiritual practice that connected all the parts of my being: physical, ethical, emotional and spiritual. Yoga embodied all of that.

Yoga does not overpower or stifle your life, it enhances it.

It gives you the tools and the freedom to use those tools.

It sharpens your vision.

It allows you to let go of what you don't need and create space for your purpose.

This ancient practice gave me profound peace. It reconnected me with the sacred truth of my own Catholic faith, as well as my humanity.

It honored who I was and where I was going.

I had no choice but to share the gift I had been given; teaching and empowering people through yoga has become my mission.

The meaning of life is to find your gift.
The purpose of life is to give it away.

—Pablo Picasso

Stage 4: The Renouncer

Ajhan Piya often told us how much easier it was to be a Renouncer than a Householder: "As a monk, I have no duties and no burdens. It's easier for me to be peaceful and meditate, because I don't have all the worries and responsibilities that you have. You have to work to make money and pay bills; my only job is to study, be your friend and help you."

There is a lot of competition in our materialistic society, lots of floating egos colliding with ours. We are of this world and, while serving our purpose, we also enjoy all of its rewards.

Even the great Renouncers like Pope Francis, Mother Teresa, Thomas Merton and the Dalai Lama have to deal with affairs of the world in order to follow their Dharma, their vision. Sitting on top of a mountain is not enough to spread peace and love any longer; we have to get down into the trenches.

So how exactly do we renounce in our modern global society?

The ultimate renunciation is not of the material but of our attachment to it.

Attachment is sometimes hard to define because, in our Western vocabulary, being attached often means *to love*. I found myself returning to my Catholic roots to comprehend that concept. As a young girl, in catechism, we learned that the ugliest sin of all was *pride* and that all other sins derived from it. We lie, we steal, we cause harm and we live with excess because we are so attached to our own self. We think we are entitled to have and do what we want because we matter more than anyone else. Simply said, the pride that my Catholic teachers warned us about is the ego.

Renunciation means death of false ego.
—Radhanath Swami

Practically, we renounce by letting go of prideful things, putting others first. As Wayne Dyer said: *Instead of asking, what's in it for me? Ask, how can I serve?*

Renouncers radiate peace, joy and humility. Like all deeply spiritual people, they love to laugh; think of the Dalai Lama's contagious giggle! They serve in the shadows, and need neither praise nor rewards. They are liberated from the demands of the ego.

Most of us will never be full-time Renouncers, but we can catch glimpses of that state in those moments when we are completely turned toward the other and forget ourselves.

For me, teaching yoga is a moment of renunciation. I belong to the people I am teaching; I don't care how I look or sound, I have no ulterior motive. I am just an instrument to serve, help and empower. I am vision in action.

Because, when you truly find yourself, you forget yourself.

* * *

I knew my spiritual journey had come full circle when I entered the Thai Buddhist temple on the other side of the James River bridge. Reflected in the golden statues of the "One who awoke," I recognized myself.

The last Herman Hesse book I had read before becoming a Householder had been *Siddharta.* I had lost it, unfinished, during one of my moves in Germany. To be truthful, I didn't like it; I don't think I even knew at the time it was the story of the Buddha.

And now, Siddharta Gautama had come back into my life.

I knew him, as I knew myself.

There was a reason why I had not finished the book; I was not ready.

This time, my soul shivered with recognition.

Searching means: having a goal. But finding means: being free, being open, having no goal.

—Herman Hesse, *Siddharta*

THE INCA TRAIL PIPER

Last spring, my husband John and I realized one of our dreams: hiking the Inca trail to Macchu Picchu. Four unforgettable days and nights at incredible altitudes challenged our bodies, fortified our minds and uplifted our souls.

The second day was the toughest, as we climbed up the highest pass on the trail: the appropriately named Dead Woman's Pass at 13,829 feet. Indeed, I felt dead a few times, taking many breaks on the unforgiving Inca steps, trying to catch my breath. I seemed to have no control over my breathing, as it heaved erratically. I felt I could never breathe normally again. The altitude forced me to confront my humanity, and with it all of my weaknesses. But the challenge also sharpened my purpose and, whatever the difficulties, I knew I would reach the top.

After a welcome and congratulatory break at the top of Dead Woman, we put our warm jackets on and started the descent to our next stop for the night, our small group scattered on the trail. John and I took our time. The steep stone steps wound their way down the wildly beautiful Andean mountains surrounded and dwarfed by snowcapped peaks. Painted across the blue skies, the forest of clouds hovered over the majestic scenery. Silence was as pure as the air.

It felt as if we were literally walking in the hand of God.

Each breath, each step a conscious echo of His presence.

Then magic happened.

A note.

Two notes.

More notes.

The sound of a flute floating from and around the mountains, the clouds and the sky all the way toward us.

The sound of a flute in the middle of nowhere.

And then we saw him, walking toward us, playing his pipe. An older native Peruvian gentleman wearing a red jacket, a hat, sandals and, around his shoulders, a small colorful woven shawl that also served as his backpack.

He greeted us and I asked him to continue playing for us.

Play for John and me, on the Inca trail, in the middle of nowhere.

He did, and then went on his way, his music gently floating away, leaving behind a sprinkling of stardust.

And a little bit of magic.

How many times, on the trail of our lives, do we encounter pipers, messengers?

How many times do we hear them, see them?

They are messengers that can only be sensed through our third eye, our intuitive intelligence, our soul.

We are too often deaf and blind to the calling of our inner voice.

We don't hear, we don't see, we don't feel what really matters when we are too occupied and distracted by the noises of the world.

We need stillness.

We need moments of our own.

We need meditation.

So, we can hear.

The Piper on the Trail of our lives.

Quiet the mind and the soul will speak.
—Ma Jaya Sati Bhagavati

6. THE THIRD EYE: AJNA CHAKRA

COLOR: Indigo or Violet
TRANSLATION: Perception, Command Point
LOCATION: Between the eyebrows

KEY WORDS: Awareness, Intuition, Imagination, Light and Dark, Visualization, Perception, Power of the Mind

RELATED BODY PARTS: Eyes, Hypothalamus (emotional processing center of the brain)

QUALITIES WHEN BALANCED: Clarity, Trusting one's Intuition, Truth, Intellectual Abilities, Learning from Experience, Openness to the Ideas of Others, Wisdom, Clairvoyance, Good Decision-Making, Mental Clarity, Non-Duality, Self-Realization

Viveka - discernment

PSYCHOLOGICAL SIGNS OF IMBALANCE: Poor Memory, Self-Doubt, Learning Disabilities, Sleep disorders, Nightmares, Lack of Concentration, Forgetfulness, Hallucinations, Delusions, Passive-Aggressiveness, "Not there", Flightiness, Lack of Imagination, Focusing on Insignificant Details instead of the Big Picture, Duality, Conflicts between Spiritual and Everyday Self

PHYSICAL SIGNS OF IMBALANCE: Hearing, Smell and Sight problems, Neurological Problems, Headaches, Strokes, Seizures, Coordination and Balance Problems

POSITIVE ARCHETYPE: The Intuitive
NEGATIVE ARCHETYPE: The Rationalist
ELEMENT: Light
SENSE: Sixth Sense
SOUND: OM

VERB: I See

FOOD: Eating consciously

HEALING TOOLS

Self-study:

- What is your vision, your gift, your true purpose?

- Have you ever been saved by your intuition?

- Reflect on the four Ashramas in your lives: which one are you in now?

- Have you been or are you on a spiritual journey?

- Have you encountered Pipers on the trail of your life?

Practical tools:

- Study great philosophers and spiritual teachers
- Sit in stillness and let yourself be guided by your intuition
- Memory Exercises
- Color Mandalas
- Keep a dream journal (when you wake up, write down your dreams. The more you study your dreams, the more clear they will be)
- Lucid Dreaming (creating our own dreams)
- Surrender to fantasy: imagine stories and fairy tales
- Wear indigo or violet clothes, have indigo or violet flowers or objects around your house
- Meditation
- Shambavi Mudra (gazing at the Third Eye)
- Star Gazing, Night Time Sky
- Nadhi Sodhana (Alternate Nostril Breathing)
- Yantra Yoga (the yoga of meditation on visual objects)

ASANAS: Eye Movements, Balancing, Forward Bends, Child's Pose

MANTRA: *I Trust the Guidance Within*

THIRD EYE MEDITATION

Find a comfortable place where you feel safe and grounded
Sitting or lying down
Relaxing into the body and into the breath
Sending the breath to the space between your eyebrows
The breath is a beautiful indigo light that nourishes and warms your
    third eye
Repeating your Mantra: *I Trust the Guidance Within*
Starting to visualize yourself walking on a dark road
So dark that you can hardly see your feet
Feeling hesitant with each step
Are you on the right path?
How would you know? It's so dark
I Trust the Guidance Within
Starting to focus on your third eye
Feeling its warm glow between your eyes
As it slowly expands into a beautiful light
Allowing you to take each step with more ease
More trust
I Trust the Guidance Within
You can see more clearly
As you look around you, you can see lights starting to flicker on your
    path
One by one
More lights
Shining bright
Your own light creating all those lights on your path
I Trust the Guidance Within
Your path is guiding you to a rocky mountain
Carved into the rock, there is a cave
Your light is leading you toward the cave
Inside the cave

Starting to walk deep into the belly of the cave
It is so dark inside
Shadows all around you, reflected on its stark walls
Are you on the right path?
I Trust the Guidance Within
Following your light
Arriving into a large room, deep into the mountain
It is filled with all you've always known and all you've always wanted to
    know
It is the cave of knowledge
The cave of wisdom
Visualizing an object in the cave of knowledge
That represents something you've always wanted to know
The one thing you most want to know
I Trust the Guidance Within
Seeing the object
Reaching for it
Holding it
Feeling yourself holding it
Feeling the infinite all-encompassing clarity of this moment
Turning around and starting to walk back
Knowing that you can find the path to the cave
The cave of Wisdom
Whenever you need to
Just following your light
I Trust the Guidance Within.

CHAPTER 7

SAHASRARA
CROWN CHAKRA

The ultimate secret: connection to all

He who experiences the unity of life sees his own self in all beings, and all beings are reflected in his own self. He looks on everything with an impartial eye.
—Buddha

Sahasrara is the state of ultimate freedom.

By realizing we are connected to all, we are able to let go of everything.

I taught a yoga class on "letting go" this morning, ending with the ubiquitous ocean music and the visualization of waves carrying away what we need to release. After class, Kevin, a fellow yogi, came up to me and shared a wonderful experience he had on the North Carolina Outer Banks a few years ago. He said he had a moment of immense clarity that day as he sat on the beach: how the ocean waves carry some of the sand away and come back for more, in an unending cycle of waves and tides. Sometimes they take more, other times they take less. But they never stop, because they are connected to a bigger picture: the sand, the water, the moon, the Earth, a beautiful unfathomable cycle that we get a glimpse of through this beautiful rhythm of the sea.

This reflects our lives so beautifully: we let go, but there's always more to let go of. We don't get it perfectly just that one time, and then all is set in stone. It's a constant ebb and flow. There is no separation, there is no end, there is just unlimited connection.

A connection that keeps flowing between itself, everything and everyone.

When you wake up to the Divine Consciousness within you and your divine identity, you wake up simultaneously to the Divine Consciousness appearing as all other beings. And this is not poetry and this is not a feeling, this is a direct experience of the divine light living in and as all other beings. And until this realization is firm in you, you do not know who or where you are.

—Andrew Harvey

THE CHALLENGE OF CONNECTION

Do not struggle. Go with the flow of things and you will find yourself at one with the mysterious unity of the universe.

—Chuang Tzu

I was not aware of this concept growing up. I saw the world only through my eyes and the dreams I had for myself.

It was my picture, my conscience, my life and, as my husband jokingly says: "The rest of us get to live in it."

It seems so simple.

The beginning and end of all.

The big secret.

But I think I have spent most of my life fighting the greatest revelation of all, that of being part of a whole, being connected to that big picture.

The big picture is not only me, but everything, everyone around me, even those I believe in my heart don't deserve it; the ones who destroy instead of creating, the ones who see the world as a playground for their own indulgences and lurk in the shadows, the users, the haters, the ones I don't want in that big picture with me.

I have grown and learned a lot through the years. I have learned to be strong through my roots, to trust my ability to let go, love and forgive. I have learned to truly know and trust myself and my decisions, but I still always felt my journey included just me and the ones I loved and perhaps, those I tolerated.

I still felt life was a fight: us against them.

Good against evil.

Love against hate.

I understand the concept of ultimate Connection. I teach it, I proclaim it, I believe in it, I embrace it as a whole, but it's still a struggle to bring it into my everyday life.

Even though I have forgiven them, I don't want to be connected to the people who have hurt me and the ones I love, to be connected to those who have harmed and are still harming the world, or to those who have no conscience, no empathy and just don't care, living lives of pure, unabandoned greed and selfishness and, in the worst cases, pure evil.

I feel I am a good person but accepting these people, loving them as part of me, is another level of good I have yet to reach.

As my Buddhist teachers taught me, it is a practice, a discipline and it is challenging. A daily struggle that we should welcome with a smile.

This smile doesn't come easily.

Just like in a Hollywood movie, I thought I would go on my hero's journey, meet hardships, fight a good fight, conquer adversity and come out stronger, surrounded by the ones I loved, while all my nemeses were locked away and sent back to another planet, pulverized into dust and surely not part of my universe ever again.

Yet the lesson is that I am connected to them. Even after learning what our encounter had to teach me, they're still here. Connected to the same beautiful Consciousness as I am.

They have as much right to it as I do.

This doesn't seem fair.

But it is part of the journey.

This is the way it is supposed to be. We have to go through all the steps of growing up, in body, mind and heart before we get a glimpse of what true Connection is.

We have to anchor ourselves into a firm reality before we can go all out and melt into the un-firm, the un-real, and the un-finite.

It is something we carefully learn one step at a time and finally mellow into, a soft pillow we can rest our head on with a sigh after a long arduous journey.

We have to build our "self" and acquire what we need before we can give.

We have to learn before we can unlearn, to be wary before we can trust and surrender completely.

It has to be difficult before it becomes easy.

SURRENDER TO UNCONDITIONAL LOVE

Love is the bridge between you and everything.

—Rumi

I caught my first glimpse of true Connection through my grandmother, Francine.

Her house was just a few steps from the village church. Up until the beginning of the twentieth century, it used to be the Sunday house of the lords of the nearby castle, who would ride there for mass and lunch afterwards. As this house fell into disrepair, the village sold it for a pittance to my grandparents, newly arrived with a brood of small children in 1942, during the German occupation.

My grandmother, a devout Catholic, spent lots of time in the church, preparing everything for the different masses—dusting, sweeping, laundering the church linen and, most of all, arranging the flowers. She would grow them and pick them from her garden and, if needed, beg my mother and uncles for some offerings from their own gardens. When there was no other alternative, she would buy them from the *fleuriste*, which infuriated my grandfather. Mémé's devotion to the *Sainte Vierge* was all encompassing; she would move heaven and earth so that the Virgin Mary always had flowers ornamenting her statue.

The tiny window to the *petite sacristie,* the room where the flowers were assembled and vases kept, opened onto the square which led to my grandparents' house. It had rusty vertical bars, set in thick Roman church walls. Every time I visited my grandparents, I would first stop at the little window. Very often, Mémé would be there, working at the wooden table amongst vases, urns, pots and fragrant bunches of—depending on the season—daisies, tulips, anemones, lilies, daffodils, asters, roses, dahlias, lilac, jasmine, baby's breath, chrysanthemums, lilies of the valley and greenery. She would be so absorbed in her task that, most of the time, she would not see me.

I loved to stand there and watch her through the bars, in her simple apron, feeling the reverence of this simple moment. It was more than the act of making bouquets; it was a communion with something greater than her, greater than me. It was an act of connection with everything she believed in, everything around her, not just in this church, but everywhere. Her gestures and her presence became infinite harmony and unconditional love. It could not be explained, but it just felt so right, as if her simple presence and actions were the answer to everything, making all the madness, troubles and aches of the world disappear. Whatever was burdening my mind at the time evaporated as I watched her and became part of All with her.

Even now, as I walk to my grandparents' house during my visits to France, now occupied by my uncle Lulu and his wife, I can't help but glance at the small window, pausing and touching the bars, trying to see inside through the glass pane now grimy with years of neglect, conjuring up the heady scents of heavy blooms and decaying greenery, and yearning for the magic of those moments watching her. No one uses this room anymore, but it is still filled with my Mémé's beautiful loving spirit and the moments she spent there, effortlessly connected to all that is.

My grandmother "got it."

She had never been taught it, she had never read about it, she had just come into it naturally.

That's why everyone loved being around her.

Because she made us feel whole.

SURRENDER TO THE MOMENT

Be here now.

—Ram Dass

My second glimpse of Connection happened in Mosjøen, Norway.

As I wrote earlier, this was one of my first real adventures, traveling by myself to the land of the Midnight Sun. I was twenty and pretty proud of myself, having conquered adversity and made what was at the time an audacious journey. My Norwegian hosts were the most hospitable people I had ever met. I was full of my own experience and learning a new language and a new culture, basking in the love of that family that would become as dear as my own.

One morning, everyone was busy so I decided to venture out by myself. I climbed the hill behind my friends' farm and started walking in the forest. There was no path and the trees were dense; I thought of turning back but kept going, until I came to what appeared to be the end of the forest. I stepped out of the woods into one the most stunning sights I had ever seen.

Because it was so unexpected.

A Gift.

A peaceful crystal blue lake right at the edge of the forest, surrounded by evergreen trees and a crisp blue sky. So clear, so blue one could not tell where the lake ended and the sky started. It was a brisk, late August morning and the sun was still burning off the residues of the night, leaving spirals of mist hovering over the surface of the water, lending the scene an eerie aura. I felt as if I was stepping into a fairy tale, a piece of what heaven looked like. And, strangely, I didn't feel like an outsider, but completely attuned to all the glory around me. Not just a spell-bound spectator, but part of the splendor.

Since then, I have learned about Vipassana—insight meditation—that moment when you're not just the observer any longer but the observed as well. That moment when there's no more duality. In that instant on the edge of that Norwegian mountain lake, I lived it.

I was the water, the trees, the sky and the clouds.

I felt whole, blissful, free and peaceful.

I don't know how long I spent up there—time had lost its relevance—but I came back down feeling different. Until then, I had been taking, taking, taking, too greedy for feelings, experiences and sensations to stop and to start connecting to something other than myself. This moment was a wake-up call that I didn't even know I needed. The image of that lake often comes back to me when I'm overwhelmed and need to find myself again.

A skeptic—me included—would say that my experience was very ordinary. After all, it's easy and normal to have one's breath taken away by the grandeur of nature. It happens all the time. Nature is mesmerizing and I've witnessed much more magnificent sights than this little Nordic lake since then, from the Grand Canyon to Costa Rican volcanoes, Ireland and Bretagne's breathtaking cliffs, pristine Caribbean beaches, the magic of Macchu Picchu and Antarctica.

But this was different. It was not about the scenery itself but about how it absorbed me and made me its own.

In that one moment, I had surrendered without even knowing it.

SURRENDER TO REVERENCE

There is a voice that doesn't use words. Listen.

—Rumi

Fifteen years later, John and I experienced one such moment together as we stood in St Peter's Square at dusk. We lived in Germany at the time and had left our three children with my parents and friends in France to tour Italy. We stayed in a small hotel near the Vatican during our three days in Rome. After a long, exhausting day walking through the city, we had freshened up at the hotel and decided to go on an evening stroll along Via Della Conciliazione toward Vatican City.

Extraordinarily, St Peter's Square, a beehive of activity during the day, was deserted. As we slowly walked deeper into the square, it felt like coming back to the womb, warm and safe, deep within the embrace of the circle of colonnades.

We stood by the Obelisk in silence, under the magical, pastel evening sky, as its hues of blues and pinks bled into the startling white of the basilica and its consort of buildings. The silence was unlike any other, it was compelling in the midst of this frantic city. It had a texture of its own. It became our silence. Something we'd been craving— again—without knowing we had.

It was not a religious moment. I honor all the facets of the religion that my grandmother exemplified as well as the beauty of its rituals that cradled my childhood. But I'm also aware of its human failings. Even though this was taking place in the epicenter of Catholic hegemony, it was bigger than the faith of my youth.

It was a universal moment, connecting to all the souls who had been stirred in that square, taken their sense of awe with them and shared it. Connecting to all other moments of the past, present and future. I felt a great love for humanity. It was not about me living this experience. It was about everyone else. Starting with the man standing beside me. I remember taking John's hand without a word and feeling that connection.

One person at a time.

As my Buddhist teachers had taught me: *Start appreciating the ones close to you before you start saving the world.*

I understood that as I returned to my real life after this vacation, I would have to take it one moment, one person at a time.

This is the only way we can handle this powerful ultimate Connection. Otherwise it will overwhelm us.

ACCIDENTS

Life will give you whatever experience is the most helpful for the evolution of your consciousness.

—Eckhart Tolle

My friend Terry asked me how we can protect ourselves as we surrender to complete compassion for all. Isn't it dangerous to connect with people who might hurt us and take advantage of our openness?

This is why I believe connection happens only when we're ready.

This is why this chakra is the last, not even inside our body, but floating over the crown of our head.

It is not something we force, it is something we allow.

We get opportunities to connect to our source throughout our lives, most of them we don't even notice. The key is to pay attention, to slow down, to remove ourselves from our own selfish needs.

Those glimpses of Connection are just accidents waiting to happen and, as Swami Satchidananda said it so well; *Yoga—or any practice of mindfulness—makes us accident-prone.*

I was lucky. My grandmother was such a powerful guiding light that I could not help but become aware of our divine connection through her. I didn't quite understand it, but I knew there was something special out there. It gave me hope.

The lake in Norway caught me at a pivotal time when I was starting to open myself to a world outside of myself and my needs. Not surprisingly, it happened in a neutral place where I felt loved and not judged.

St Peter's Square was the right place and moment for me to reconnect. I had lost some of my inner light after my brother died. I held anger and resentment in my heart for the world that took him away from us. That evening brought me back to Trust.

There have been many other moments since then, simple moments that have brought a smile to my soul and made challenging times bearable.

The Buddha tells us that separation is what causes suffering. As we accept the truth of our Connection to All, we come into the realization that all the love, power, joy and infinite potential of our source are also within us.

The more we surrender, we more we connect.

The more we connect, we more open we are to the lessons awaiting us.

One drop at a time.

I am not just the single drop in the ocean; I am the ocean in the drop.

—Rumi

SURRENDER TO EMPATHY

*Until we extend the circle of our compassion to all living things,
humanity will not know peace.*

—Albert Schweitzer

I was stuck.

This book was written and edited, Terry had finished the beautiful painting that would be my cover, but I was struggling with the business part of this project, uncertain of the next step. The typed manuscript was resting in the cubbyhole above my desk, as I let other priorities take precedence over the final essential part of this journey. Release it!

Writing was easy.

But publishing had become a dirty, scary word.

This final surrender was hard. I was afraid to mess up and be rejected. I didn't have a media presence, neither blog nor webpage and definitely not enough Instagram followers. I just wanted someone to take my book and put it out there, even though I knew that those final steps into the unknown had to be mine. And mine only.

Then, the universe sent me a messenger.

An adorable messenger with curly blond hair. My daughter.

"Mama, do you want to go and see Oprah?"

Oprah was coming to New York to film her Super Soul Conversations at the Apollo Theater the following week. Oprah had been my inspiration ever since, after moving in with John, I saw her on the American Forces Network's one and only channel in Germany. I had never seen anyone on television before talk about spirit without referring to the Holy Spirit. Here was someone who spoke my language. I always thought I was weird, but I realized then that many others were just as weird and thirsty for meaning as I was. Right now, she was just what I needed; if anyone could give me the final boost to release my work, she was the one. I booked my train ticket to the Big Apple and, on a snowy New York day, I went to see Oprah in Harlem with my daughter.

On her first interview with Jordan Peele, I heard her say what I was meant to hear:

Stories bring connection and connection brings empathy.

Right there was my missing link.

My "aha!" moment, as she likes to call it.

My stories were part of universal connection. I could choose to keep them stuck in their folder in the cubbyhole above my desk, or I could be brave and release them.

My stories did not really belong to me. Just like anyone's stories, they were part of the universal flow of consciousness, part of the beautiful web of life that wrapped us into its amazing embrace but also took us on wild rides between peaks and valleys, part of the cycle of seasons, night and day, birth and rebirth. My stories would connect you to your own stories, past, present and future. My stories, just like yours, were nothing by themselves, but when they connected, they became alive, they became extraordinary. They became a vehicle for empathy.

As Oprah uttered those words, one vivid image popped into my mind.

We were standing next to a fence. An odd gathering: Papa, three older gentlemen, and me, with a one-year-old France-Lee balanced on my hip. It was September 1987 and we were in Tann, near Fulda, West Germany, a few feet from the Iron Curtain, the epicenter of the Cold War, separation between East and West.

Papa had always refused to come and see us in Germany, a country of *sales Boches,* as he called Germans, people he despised because he believed they had destroyed his family. He finally relented that summer when he heard we would soon be moving to the United States, and drove eight hours to Hanau, where we lived outside of Frankfurt, with Maman.

During their week with us, I took them to Fulda—it was a two-hour drive but I wanted them to see the infamous Iron Curtain. There were a few other people in the spot where we parked: three older gentlemen, all speaking German, looking with binoculars at what seemed to be a small village tuckered behind the Eastern no man's land zone—a field of weeds—on the other side. I was observing Papa; he had been complaining about the long drive and I was wary this could trigger a violent public outburst against Germans. Instead he came up to me and made this strange request: "Could I use your interpreting skills? I'd like to speak with those people and ask them questions."

He asked them what they were looking at, where they were during the war. They told him they had family on the other side: a sister, aunts, uncles and cousins, that they had not seen since the division of their country. Two of them had fought in the war as very young men, they did not have a choice. Just like Papa, they had lost and suffered. They talked for almost an hour. I was the conduit between their stories, keenly aware that healing was happening. When it was over, they shook hands. As we walked back to the car, Papa turned to me and said: "They're just like us. They've been through a lot too."

All it took were a few stories to connect him to the people he had hated for so long. Their narratives had helped him feel their pain, and realize that it matched his own; their hearts beat to the same rhythm as his.

The most important revelation is that connection and empathy are not the culmination of our journey. It's not the end of the road, or cul-de-sac, as we say in French; literally the ass of a bag.

No, that bag is bottomless.

Empathy is bottomless, infinite.

And once you've found that ultimate connection, you've also found that ultimate surrender. Surrender to the call of action.

You cannot do nothing.

It's not about what yoga can do for you, but about approaching your practice in the spirit of offering.

—Shiva Rea

And here goes the magical circle of yoga and the chakras. As we reach Sahasrara, we don't stay there; we understand the need to go back to Muladhara, to the roots, to the earth, to dig our hands into the dirt. We understand the need to do the work or, as the Buddha said, go to the market place.

It's easy to be peaceful on our embroidered meditation cushions in front of our altars decorated with our little trinkets, in our yoga studios, with the dimmed lights and the soothing music, on the top of our mountains or during our exotic retreats. But we need to remember that this is just practice, preparing us for the real world and real action.

We know we've got it when we want to give back.

We know we've got it when we want to act, when we want to move.

When you pray, move your feet.

—African proverb

SURRENDER TO SACRED ACTION

Unless our fundamental sacred connectedness with every being and thing is experienced deeply and enacted everywhere, religious, political, and other differences will go on creating intolerable conflict that can only increase the already dangerously high chances of our self-annihilation.

—Andrew Harvey

Coming back from New York, I finally understood that I was not ready to release this book because it was not finished.

Just like I had to surrender my stories to the world, I had to emphasize that yoga's surrender to divine consciousness is ultimately a surrender to action. All our physical and spiritual work prepares us for intentional work in the real world.

My teacher Rolf Gates told us this story during one of my yoga trainings. He had received a revelation in, of all places, an airport lavatory. The flushing system was complicated so a sign explained how it worked: pull up and then pull down. He realized that this was the ultimate principle of yoga: you pull up into the spiritual world but you pull it back down into the physical world.

Without pulling back down, yoga doesn't flow, it's stagnant.

Just another self-involved activity.

Yoga is putting your Self out there.

Yoga flows, yoga connects.

You're constantly pulling up and pulling down.

Yoga occurs when our inner work manifests in the world around us.

—Michael Stone

Service effortlessly brings me back to Muladhara. Helping others is firmly established in my roots. I come from a long line of volunteers who did service for the church, the poor, the sick, the elderly, the community and the world. As a very young child, I was delivering *La Vie Catholique* for my grandmother, and selling chocolate eggs for her Easter fundraiser. My entire family helped at the annual village flea market—its biggest fundraiser—with three generations of women proudly working my grandmother's waffle-maker. I always thought that all dishes had a sticker with the owner's name on it because most dishes in my family were marked that way, as they were as much a part of the communal merry-go-round of sharing as of our cupboards.

I have volunteered since then for military families, my children's schools, my church, refugees and my community. My children have continued this tradition, hopefully not just as followers of a family tradition, but as citizens of the world. Because we all need to step out of our comfort zone. Our world needs us to act big.

We're walking each other home.

—Ram Dass

As a yoga seeker and teacher, I have become aware of the need to step out of my own little bubble. Speak up for what I believe, be an activist. I feel the urge to bring my spiritual work to life around me. It's not enough to talk about spirit and connection, I have to be a link myself to restore connectedness where I see separation in the world.

I care about the Earth deeply and I am willing to take action for the environment, not just with my words, but with my reduced consumerism and my voice.

I care for the poor and our children's future and I am willing to support the people who are out there in the trenches. For example, my friend who is running for office on behalf of those who have no voice and no influence, and the public figures who work toward connection instead of division.

I care for justice and am willing to champion beautiful human beings like my friend Nadine who, after her first trip to India, decided she couldn't go back to her regular life after learning that the birth land of yoga and the Buddha had the largest concentration of children trafficked into sex slavery. She has since then dedicated her life and her yoga to this cause.

Making my meditations about the world.

Inspiring others to do the same.

Because this is where we truly find ourselves.

Out in the marketplace.

And we each have a special role to play in that marketplace.

Yoga provides us with a guideline for how to live in the world as if it was our very self because ... there is no separation. A body of water cannot vote and neither can a rain forest. Yoga challenges us to move into the world guided by nonviolent means and remain grounded in a spiritual practice rooted in honest and responsive action.

—Michael Stone

* * *

The Bodhisattva

My Buddhist teachers taught me the story of the Bodhisattva, who exemplifies spirit in action. She is a being who has reached enlightenment but will not rest in Nirvana until everyone else has also found enlightenment. The real Bodhisattva identifies the immeasurable distress of all beings as her own. The eradication of her own suffering is joined with the desire to aid in the eradication of all others' suffering as well. She chooses to come back into the world to be of service, in whatever capacity she is needed.

This is the Bodhisattva prayer performed each morning by his Holiness the Dalai Lama:

May I be a guard for those who need protection
A guide for those on the path
A boat, a raft, a bridge for those who wish to cross the flood
May I be a lamp in the darkness
A resting place for the weary
A healing medicine for all who are sick
A vase of plenty, a tree of miracles
And for the boundless multitudes of living beings
May I bring sustenance and awakening
Enduring like the earth and sky
Until all beings are freed from sorrow
And all are awakened.

* * *

Last month, I read this prayer at the end of a very long weekend of yoga training. I was feeling the way I usually do at the end of those weekends: exhausted, drained but also blissful from having given everything I had to give to help my students on their journey. As I was cleaning up, a young woman, Eleni who had impressed me throughout the course with her sensitivity to the world suffering and her altruistic commitment to help the less privileged, came up to me and said those beautiful words: "I think *you* are a Bodhisattva!" My first instinct was to vehemently negate her generous comment, as I come from a long generation of women unable to take a compliment. But I remembered the words of my teacher Ajahn Piya when someone asked him if he knew any Bodhisattvas. He said that we all got glimpses and chances of being one, even for a brief moment. So instead of brushing off her kind words, I received them, smiled and said: "Thank you, I think you are one too."

The light in me honors the light in you. Namaste!

Each of us carries a Bodhisattva within.
The ultimate choice to connect with her is ours.

Music in the soul can be heard by the universe.

—Lao-Tzu

7. THE CROWN CHAKRA: SAHASRARA

COLOR: Crystal White Light or Violet
TRANSLATION: Thousand-fold, Infinity
LOCATION: Crown of the head

KEY WORDS: Understanding, Knowing, Transcendence, Immanence, Spirituality

RELATED BODY PARTS: Brain, Cellular and Genetic Level, Cerebral Cortex, Central Nervous System

QUALITIES WHEN BALANCED: Unity Consciousness, Connection to our Source, Harmony, Sense of Oneness, Bliss, Ability to Surrender

PSYCHOLOGICAL SIGNS OF IMBALANCE: Disturbances caused by any Sense of Separation, Depression, Alienation, Confusion, Boredom, Bigotry, Inability to Learn, Overly Intellectual, Spacey

PHYSICAL SIGNS OF IMBALANCE: Identifying with physical illness as Me or Mine

POSITIVE ARCHETYPE: The Guru
NEGATIVE ARCHETYPE: The Egocentric
ELEMENT: Consciousness, Cosmic Universality
SENSE: Primordial Knowing
SOUND: The Soundless Sound of Consciousness within
VERB: We are
FOOD: Prana (Life Force)

HEALING TOOLS

Self-study:

- What makes you feel connected to All?

- Is it difficult for you to feel connected to your Source?

- Do you have a regular spiritual practice?

- Remember a special time when you felt complete Surrender to Unconditional Love

- Remember a special time when you felt complete Surrender to the Moment

- Remember a special time when you felt complete Surrender to Reverence

- What does Empathy mean to you? How does it manifest in your life?

- What part does Service play in your life?

- What does Sacred Action mean to you?

Practical tools:
- Study your spiritual culture, tradition
- Study another spiritual tradition/religion and adopt one of their practices that would enhance your own practice
- See all the common points between religions: One Truth Many Paths
- Take a class in something spiritually or intellectually stimulating
- Experience Nature in a way that makes you feel connected
- Go to the mountains, climb to a mountain top
- Pray, write an invocation or prayer
- Fast for one day
- Wear white, and decorate your house with white flowers, linen or objects
- Do nothing for one day and spend it in meditation or contemplation
- Go on a retreat
- Meditation (Vipassana)
- Guided Imagery
- Energy Healing

ASANAS: Seated or moving meditation, any pose that makes you feel connected

MANTRA: *I Am Connected to All*

CROWN CHAKRA MEDITATION

Find a comfortable place where you feel safe and grounded
Sitting or lying down
Relaxing into the body and into the breath
Sending the breath to the crown of your head
The breath is a beautiful white light that nourishes and warms the
    crown of your head
Repeating your Mantra: *I Am Connected to All*
Starting to visualize yourself laying down in a meadow
Feeling so peaceful
I Am Connected to All
Your body feels so relaxed
As if it was resting on a soft fluffy cloud
Visualizing the white fluffy cloud under your body
Feeling so light
So light that your body on the white cloud starts rising
Rising above the meadow
Higher into the blue sky
Until you're among the clouds
I Am Connected to All
Sitting up on your white fluffy cloud
Looking around you at the sea of clouds
So white, almost translucent in the luminosity of the sun
I Am Connected to All
Looking down at the world beneath you
The snow-capped mountains and the rolling hills
The vast oceans and the sinuous rivers
The majestic waterfalls and the placid lakes
The fields, the gardens and the parks, alive with colors
The big cities and their crests of skyscrapers
The small towns and their marketplaces
The caravans, the mobile homes, the tents, the huts, the caves

I Am Connected to All

The churches, the mosques, the temples, the synagogues, the altars in
the woods

I Am Connected to All

All the dwellings and all the people inside the dwellings

I Am Connected to All

All races, all ages, all colors, all creeds and nationalities

I Am Connected to All

Sitting on your cloud, feeling at one with the world beneath you, the
world around you and the world within you

I Am Connected to All

OM.

EPILOGUE

Our journey is not a straight road; it weaves and turns, and often snakes back on itself, seemingly bringing us back to the starting point.

We constantly move from chakra to chakra, creating and filling voids and blocks.

Space and Notes.

We create a symphony.

The symphony of our lives.

* * *

THE FABLE OF THE SEVEN NOTES

by Christine Griggs

The world was a sad place.

A place without music.

Ages ago, the Seven Notes had a disagreement about which one of them was the most important. People took sides, debated and, when no agreement could be reached, each Note went its separate way. Each trying to make its own music, a pitiful one-note creation.

The world was a very sad place.

One long summer afternoon in the mountains, a young shepherd, sitting among his flock, was playing with a stick that he had whittled into a flute. His grandparents had told him about this beautiful fusion of sounds that was called music. They had said that there was nothing like it; it brought joy to your heart, a smile to your face and lightness to your step. The world had lost its true music because of pride and ego. Now music was reduced to a single note. The same note that piteously lilted out of his flute, a sad echo of the bleating of his sheep.

His grandparents had told him that true music was made out of the connection of the Seven Notes, now scattered across the universe. Only true selflessness could bring those Notes together. And, just like music, selflessness was lacking in the world. Everyone was too busy trying to sound louder than everyone else to worry about connecting with other sounds.

The young shepherd made a decision; he would visit each of the Seven Notes and beg them to make peace and reconnect. Beg them to make music again.

He announced his decision to his family and embarked on his journey.

His first visit was to *Do*'s red cave, deep into the earth. When he found her, she was taking a mud bath. She welcomed him and insisted on feeding him as she listened to his plea: "Music needs you; it starts with you. You're its foundation and what keeps it grounded." *Do* was a nurturer, and extremely reliable, so it didn't take long to convince her. She was attached to her home, but she was also fearless and told the shepherd she would accompany him and protect him on his journey.

Re lived in the middle of the sea. They had to take a boat to reach her home. When they called her name, she emerged from the water, a nude vision of glistening, long orange hair and limbs. She tried to entice them with sensual pleasures, inviting them to swim with her and let the water massage their weary bodies. She worked her wiles to persuade them to stay. But the shepherd did not relent: "Music needs you; you're what gives it fluidity and emotions, you allow it to connect to all our senses. Think of how many people you can touch if you unite with the other Notes." *Re* thrived on relationships and she had been very lonely, missing her intimacy with the other Notes, so she conceded and joined them.

Mi lived in a volcano. They had to trek up to its top and stand at the edge of the crater to meet him. When he emerged, he was engulfed in bright yellow fire. "What do you want?" he roared. *Mi* exuded power, which could lead to pride and an exaggerated sense of self, so the shepherd had to tread carefully: "Music needs you; you're the energy that gives it its purpose, but you're also the discipline that keeps it going." *Mi* was flattered, but what guided his decision to follow them was his sense of commitment; he had no doubt at all that his strength was needed.

Fa lived in a huge, green air balloon, floating among the clouds. The shepherds and the three Notes hired their own balloon to visit her. Reaching *Fa* was not easy; she was between the earth and the sky, the body and the soul. She was that heart energy centered between what grounds the notes and what uplifts them. She welcomed them with a warm smile and open arms, but she expressed misgivings at the shepherd's words: "Music needs you; you are the compassion and generosity that gives it its heart." Her smile became sorrowful: "I wanted us to stay together, and I was so hurt when we went our separate ways. I don't know if I can trust again." But forgiveness was stronger than resentment, and she steered her balloon to follow theirs.

So lived in the ether, higher up in the clouds. He had been the most expressive in their battle for dominance, and the most affected by their split. When they reached his home, they could hardly distinguish his ethereal blue shape from the blue of the skies around him. Silence surrounded him and the shepherd's voice trembled a little when he made his plea: "Music needs you; you are its voice and the one who expresses its vibrant creative spirit." *So* broke his silence, anger simmering in his words: "I Am Sound. Without me, there is no music, just ideas and dreams. I am the one who brings dreams to life. I am the most important part of Music." The shepherd let silence set in once again, feeling the restlessness of the four other Notes behind him before he spoke: "You are right; there is no music without you. But there is also no music without the other six Notes. You have been without them for so long now. What music have you created with the Sound that you own?" Once more, he let silence settle. "Tell me, what is the use of a voice if it has nothing to say?" *So* let out his one single note of despair and nodded: "I have wasted so much time, and let so much be unsaid." He led the way as the two balloons followed his blue shape higher into the heavens.

La lived in light. They followed one dazzling ray as it shot from the sun and then beamed down onto the surface of a lake, transforming it into a pool of violet. *La* surrounded them and they felt his presence as clearly as if they could see him. They heard him whisper: "I knew you would come, I have been waiting for you." As this unspoken voice affirmed the intent of his quest, the shepherd sighed with relief: "Music needs you; you are the intuition that guides the flow of its notes, the clarity that guides its rhythm and the affirmation that it is just as it should be." *La* mellowed into a softer light and they saw themselves through his eyes, mirrored into the lake, as his breath carried his words: "I have been blinded by my own light and I could not see what really mattered. What's the point of having so much wisdom if I don't use it, to know all if I don't share it? I have been a light without a spectrum, a spectrum without a rainbow. I am coming home."

They didn't have to go search for *Ti*; she had been here all along. *Ti* knew she didn't exist without the others. But she also knew she was the one that added that "little something" which took music from mundane to transcendent. Some pieces of music could actually exist without her touch, but they were mediocre, short-lived, meant to crash into oblivion. Ti added spirit to the notes. *Ti* was the link with the universal vibration, the Music above us. She removed all barriers and all separations. *Ti* was the mistress of Oneness, she made it all possible. The shepherd didn't have to utter the words; *Ti* had already heard them. She was already with them around the lake as they gathered into a circle and became one again.

People who lived nearby would later tell stories of seeing a full-circled rainbow over the lake and inside the lake. One could not tell the difference between the rainbow and its reflection.

There was no difference.

Finally reunited, the Seven Notes exhaled together, blending all their sounds into one.

Then, they all stopped.

It didn't sound right.

It was music, but it didn't sound right.

The shepherd lowered his head in despair; he had traveled the universe to bring the Seven Notes together, but this had not been enough. Something was missing, something he had not found.

Do came to him and took his hand: "We cannot recreate true music. Something is missing and this missing part has been guiding us all along. It is what brought us together, what helped us make sense of the cacophonic mess we had made. It is the most important part of Music, what gives it its soul. It is Space. And it is right here. Come and join us, *Espace!*"

Espace pulled his flute out of his pocket and brought it to his lips. Surrounded by the Seven Notes, he played.

Magic happened.

Music was back.

And the world was happy again.

La Musique est l'Espace entre les Nôtes.

Music is the Space between the Notes.

—Claude Debussy

YOGA WITH YOUR OWN TWIST

Write Your Own Chakra Journey

Yoga is the journey of the Self through the Self to the Self.
—The Bhagavad Gita

MULADHARA CHAKRA
Treasure Your Roots

- Dandelions: parts of your roots you want to forget
- Your shelters
- Story of survival in your life
- Lavender ice-cream: what makes your history/heritage special?

SVADHISHTHANA CHAKRA
Some Relationships are Forever, Some are for a Season

- Trying to fit in
- Childhood friends
- Special friendships
- Your rock
- Your children (if applicable)
- Angels
- Soul buddies
- Stars in your sky

MANIPURA CHAKRA
Do Not Surrender Your Power to Others

- Judgment in your life
- Courage in your life
- Your quiet battle
- Risks you took to blossom
- Your four suitcases

ANAHATA CHAKRA
Just Forgive

- Your Count of Monte Cristo story
- The greatest tragedy in your life
- From pain to forgiveness: 4 steps
  - Easy Love
  - A good life
  - Stop being so righteous
  - Let go of expectations
- Your Bastille Day: time to recommit to forgiveness

VISHUDDHA CHAKRA
The Thought Manifests as the Word

- Thoughts that have defined your life
- Ask your loved ones what thoughts have defined their lives
- The power of words in your life: when you have to decide between *Ahimsa* (non-hurting) and *Satya* (Truth)
- Do you know a *Corbeau*?
- Deeds that make you come alive

- What is your snake whistle: the voice within you begging to be heard?

AJNA CHAKRA
Trust Your Intuition

- Red light green light moments in your life
- Amber light moments in your life
- A road into the dark woods: one example when your intuition saved you
- Describe the 4 Ashramas/stages that pertain to your life:
    - The Student
    - The Householder
    - The Forest-Dweller
    - The Renouncer
- The Piper on the trail of your life: a messenger that appeared in your life

SAHASRARA CHAKRA
The Ultimate Secret: Connection to All

- How do you comprehend the concept of Connection? Is it challenging?
- Your example of Surrender to Unconditional Love
- Your example of Surrender to the Moment
- Your example of Surrender to Reverence
- Glimpses of Connection are Accidents:
    - Have you been accident-prone?
    - Recall some of those accidents.
- Your example of Surrender to Empathy
- Your example of Surrender to Sacred Action

- The Bodhisattva within you

Yoga is a way to move into stillness in order to experience the truth of who you are... It is a matter of listening inwardly for guidance all the time, and then daring enough... And trusting enough...
To do as you are prompted to do.

—Eric Schiffmann

ACKNOWLEDGMENTS

If the only prayer you ever say in your entire life is thank you, it will be enough.
—Meister Eckhart

This book was inside of me for thirty years. My yoga practice and my fellow travelers have helped me bring it to the surface. I am feeling infinite gratitude for all of you.

Thank you to my husband John and my children France-Lee, JC and Patou; they are my guiding lights and make everything possible with their love and honesty.

Thank you to my parents and grandparents; their courage and integrity have made me who I am today.

Thank you to my yoga students whose transformation through their yoga journey has inspired and humbled me. Thank you for your dedication and invaluable support for the past eleven years.

Liz, thank you for relentlessly asking me to join your writing group. I'm so glad I finally said yes. I was afraid to be judged; instead I was empowered.

Terry, thank you for being my editing partner, your patience reading the same chapters over and over, and for painting so exquisitely the vision I had for my cover.

Thank you both for holding me accountable and for your encouragement when I doubted myself.

Carol, thank you for your unwavering support and faith in me, and for proofreading my entire manuscript three times.

Elaine, thank you for your editing skills and your poetic insight.

Michelle, thank you for being my cheerleader and teaching me to accept compliments.

Salome, thank you for your loving support and presence.

Thank you to my soul buddies; you know who you are.

Thank you to the monks of Wat Pasantidhamma: Ajhan Piya, Montre and Udhom, who have helped me to meditate and walk lightly.

Thank you to all my yoga teachers and my yoga community.

Thank you to my little bunny FuzzBuzz who became paralyzed and passed as I was finishing this book; this gentle soul was a kindred spirit who calmed me, loved me unconditionally, and gave me soft bunny kisses until his final breath. He reminded me that yoga, life, and this book, is about infinite love.

BIBLIOGRAPHY

I cannot live without books.

—Thomas Jefferson

When I read a book… now and then I come across a passage, perhaps only a phrase, which has a meaning for me, and it becomes part of me.

—Somerset W. Maugham

Wheels of Life, by Judith Anodea
Anatomy of Spirit, by Caroline Myss
The Yoga Sutras of Patanjali, Sri Swami Satchidananda
The Secret Power of Yoga, by Nischala Joy Devi
When Things Fall Apart, by Pema Chodron
Change your Thoughts, Change your Life, by Wayne Dyer
Yoga for a World out of Balance, by Michael Stone
The Direct Path, by Andrew Harvey
Meditations from the Mat, by Rolf Gates
The Collected Poems of Rumi
Siddharta, by Herman Hesse
Steppenwolf, by Herman Hesse

Read not to contradict and confute… nor to find talk and discourse, but to weigh and consider.

—Sir Francis Bacon

ABOUT THE AUTHOR

Christine Griggs was born and raised in the beautiful Bugey region of France. She studied in England and Germany and traveled the world with her American husband and their three children before settling down in Virginia in 1998. She is a multilingual translator and an ERYT-500 yoga teacher and trainer. With yoga, she found the universal language that would help her on her mission: to empower others to find the music within them and share it with the world. Her trainings include Yoga Fit, the Swami Satchidananda Integral Yoga 200-hour training and Rolf Gates' 500-hour Advanced Vinyasa Training. Her specialties are Vinyasa, Yin and Chair Yoga.

Her classes are inspirational and provide a safe caring environment, as well as a mindful rejuvenating practice interwoven with yogic principles that empower her students to live the lives they are meant to live. She teaches yoga classes, workshops and trains yoga teachers in Virginia, where she lives with her husband John. She is still traveling the world with him and enjoys learning, writing, running, hiking and sitting in her meditation garden listening to the sounds of nature. She is living her life to the rhythm of Rumi's quote: *Allow the beauty of what you love to become what you do.* She is currently working on a book of yoga poems and themes, as well as a fantasy novel based on the chakras.

You can find out more at www.yintraveler.com

ABOUT THE ILLUSTRATOR

I had a vision for my cover: French shutters opening onto a field of lavender—an invitation for the reader to sit in a comfortable chair and enjoy my book, my Tibetan bowl on the coffee table a tangible link between my French roots and my yoga path. Terry brought my idea to life more perfectly than I could have imagined.

Terry Cox-Joseph divides her time between writing and painting. She has a BFA in illustration from Minneapolis College of Art and Design. Her work appears on greeting cards, book covers, and websites. She is a member of the Poetry Society of Virginia and National League of American Pen Women, and is a former newspaper reporter and editor. For ten years she was the coordinator for the annual Christopher Newport University Writers' Conference and Contest. She derives inspiration from her family, her pets, and her three acres where she lives on a creek near the James River.

You can see more of her work at www.terrycoxjoseph.com

THE STORY CONTINUES...

In March of this year, I was coming out of a yoga class when this Facebook message popped on my screen: "Bonjour, I'm searching for my cousin Christine G. Her dad's name was Marcel and her mom's Thérèse. Is there any chance that this could be you?"

Ever since I can remember, I've had this longing for reconnection with this lost part of myself; the mystery that was my father and his family. And here it was, a call from the other side of the ocean from a cousin I had never met.

David is the son of my father's younger sister. After his mother died, David inherited a box of letters and photos that belonged to our grandmother. Last year, he felt a need to go through that box, where he found letters from my mom and photos of me, my brother and my father. He felt compelled to search for me and found me on Facebook on his first attempt.

What a blessing to finally meet—even though it was only through messages and phone calls—a cousin who knew my paternal family history and the details of that tragedy that changed my father's life. Before the war, they were a loving happy united family. My father was the strong one and very protective of his siblings who adored him. Over the years, my grandmother talked about him, my brother and me every day and her heart ached from missing us. She was very kind, generous and very spiritual. David also described his mother's irrational fits of anger that matched my father's. All their lives, both siblings relived the same nightmares separately when they could have supported each other. The lesson is that we can mend the past and reconnect, as David and I have. Our long conversations have made us realize how alike we are and

I plan to meet him and his lovely family in the suburbs of Paris during my next visit to France.

Stories are about connection and empathy, and I truly believe that releasing my story into the world helped us to find each other.

* * *

Thank you for reading my book and allowing me to share my journey with you. I hope it helps you on your own path. Please send me feedback and share your experience with me. I would love to hear from you. You can contact me, read my blogs and news of upcoming book releases, and join my community of Yin Travelers on www.yintraveler.com.

I am currently putting together a children's book based on the *Fable of the Seven Notes* featured in the epilogue of this book.

I'm also working on a volume of Yoga Poems and Themes, as well as a fantasy novel based on the chakras, creating a mystical world vibrating to the rhythm of the chakras, their colors, sensations, human and spiritual connections, adventures and wisdom.

Please leave a helpful review at Amazon.
This will help spread the word about this book.
Merci!

Made in the USA
Middletown, DE
28 December 2018